Sculpting The Mindset
Navigating Life with a Winning Mindset Unlocking Your Potential for Success

by

N. K. Sondhi

Sculpting The Mindset
Navigating Life with a Winning Mindset
Unlocking Your Potential for Success
by N. K. Sondhi

ISBN: 978-93-61150-88-3

Published by

DOUBLE 9 BOOKS

2/13-B, Ansari Road
Daryaganj, New Delhi – 110002
info@double9books.com
www.double9books.com
Tel. 011-40042856

ABOUT THE AUTHOR

In the captivating pages of "Sculpting Your Minds," the author, a seasoned retired banker, unveils a profound exploration of the intricate landscapes of the human mind. With a career marked by navigating the financial intricacies of thousands of customers, the author has acquired a unique understanding of the diverse mindset of people across various strata of society. The author's pen has been a powerful instrument, contributing to the literary landscape with more than 15 thought-provoking books that serve as beacons illuminating the shadows of contemporary social issues. Each tome penned by this insightful author reflects a commitment to unravelling the complexities of society, shedding light on matters ranging from economic inequality and social justice to community resilience and interpersonal dynamics. "Sculpting Your Minds" is a testament to the author's multifaceted expertise, combining the financial acumen garnered during a distinguished banking career with a keen awareness of the broader social fabric. This book is not merely a singular addition to the author's impressive body of work; it is a culmination of a literary journey that has consistently sought to engage readers in critical reflections on the world we inhabit. Whether exploring the nuances of financial decision-making or dissecting the intricacies of societal challenges, the author's unique ability to distil complex issues into accessible narratives has made each book a compelling read. Through this extensive literary portfolio, the author has earned a reputation as a perceptive commentator on the human condition, urging readers to contemplate, question, and ultimately, strive for positive change. As readers embark on the pages of "Sculpting Your Minds," they are not only invited to explore the author's latest contribution to the literary realm but also encouraged to delve into a rich tapestry of perspectives woven across the entirety of a remarkable literary career-one that continues to shape conversations on the social issues that define our times.

CONTENTS

Disclaimer...7

Preface..8

CHAPTER 1
WHAT IS MINDSET 10

CHAPTER 2
PSYCHOLOGY OF MINDSET 13

CHAPTER 3
 HUMAN EMOTIONS THAT INFLUENCE OUR MIND 26

CHAPTER 4
IMPACT OF WORRY & HOW TO MANAGE IT 46

CHAPTER 5
EGO AND ATTITUDE 51

CHAPTER 6
STRUGGLES IN LIFE 66

CHAPTER 7
HEALTH...79

CHAPTER 8
IMPACT OF MOTIVATION ON OUR MINDSET 88

CHAPTER 9
WILL POWER..94

CHAPTER 10
INTELLIGENCE..99

CHAPTER 11
REASONING 105

CHAPTER 12
PERCEPTION 111

CHAPTER 13
IMPACT OF IMAGINATION ON OUR MINDSET 116

CHAPTER 14
FIGURING OUT OURSELVES 122

CHAPTER 15
IDENTITY...128

CHAPTER 16
STRESS..133

CHAPTER 17
EVENTS OF PAST, PRESENT AND FUTURE....................................140

CHAPTER 18
HOW TO TACKLE MINDSET 146

Disclaimer

This book, "Sculpting the Mind: Crafting a Masterpiece of Thoughts, Emotions, and Connections," is a compilation of insights from various sources, including personal reflections, artificial intelligence, and external references. The information presented within these pages is intended for the purpose of exploration, self-discovery, and personal growth.

It is crucial to note that the perspectives, interpretations, and recommendations provided in this book are not a substitute for professional advice. Drawing on diverse sources, the author has strived to create a resource that stimulates thoughtful contemplation and encourages introspection.

Readers should approach the content with an open mind, recognizing that the ideas presented may vary based on individual experiences and perspectives. This book does not claim to provide universal solutions to the complexities of the human mind, and it intends to complement, not replace, professional guidance when necessary.

The author acknowledges the dynamic nature of the information landscape, and external sources referenced in this book may be subject to updates or changes. While efforts have been made to ensure accuracy, readers are encouraged to verify information from the original sources, especially in rapidly evolving fields.

By engaging with "Sculpting the Mind," readers acknowledge that the book is not a substitute for professional advice, and the author and publisher are not liable for any consequences resulting from applying the ideas and insights contained herein. Personal experiences and interpretations may vary, and readers are encouraged to seek individualized guidance when needed.

As you embark on this journey of self-discovery, may the amalgamation of insights from various sources enrich your exploration into the fascinating landscape of the human mind.

Preface

In the delicate art of crafting "Sculpting the Mind: Crafting a Masterpiece of Thoughts, Emotions, and Connections," I find myself standing at the intersection of curiosity and introspection. This preface serves as a personal guidepost, a glimpse into the genesis of this exploration into the realms of the mind.

As a fellow traveller on the path of self-discovery, I'm at the intricate tapestry of human thoughts, the kaleidoscope of emotions, and the profound significance of connections that shape the contours of our lives. The inspiration for this book stems from the belief that understanding the mind is akin to being an artist, sculpting our perceptions and experiences into a unique masterpiece.

Each chapter is a brushstroke, painting a picture of the sculptor's journey through the studio of self-awareness. Drawing from personal experiences, shared stories, and the collective wisdom of introspective minds, "Sculpting the Mind" is not just a compilation of insights but a shared exploration of the human condition.

In this preface, I thank those who paved the way for this introspective odyssey. To the mentors who imparted lessons in resilience, the friends who shared their stories of connection, and the countless thinkers who illuminated the nuances of the human mind — the collective wisdom shapes the narrative of this book.

I sincerely express my gratitude to Ms. Jahnvi Khanna for the exceptional support she provided for this book. Working alongside a counsellor specializing in psychology, criminology, and mental health brought invaluable insights and expertise to the project. Ms. Khanna's guidance played a crucial role in enhancing the accuracy and depth of the book's contents.

It is crucial to recognize and appreciate Ms. Jahnavi Khanna's effort in assisting me with every chapter of this book. Collaborative endeavours consistently lead to a more well-rounded and informed piece of writing.

As you turn the pages, consider this a guide and a dialogue. The sculptor's journey is as much yours as it is mine. Together, let us delve into the intricacies of thoughts, the depths of emotions, and the beauty of connections. May this exploration be a catalyst for your own artistic endeavour in sculpting the masterpiece that is your life.

CHAPTER 1
WHAT IS MINDSET

The mind is like the control centre of your thoughts, feelings, and actions. It's a bit like a supercomputer in your head that helps you understand the world around you and make decisions. Imagine it's made up of different parts, just like a car has an engine, wheels, and brakes. Similarly, your mind has parts that help you think, remember, feel emotions, and make choices.

When you see, hear, or experience something, your mind stores that information in different 'folders,' just like you store photos or files on a computer. These 'folders' help you remember things when you need them.

For example, your mind helps you remember your favourite food, how to ride a bike, or the name of your best friend.

The mind also controls your emotions. Like a weather forecast, sometimes you feel happy like when the sun is shining, and sometimes you might feel sad or angry like when there's a storm. Your mind helps you understand and deal with these feelings.

When you have to decide, your mind sorts through all the information collected and helps you choose what to do. Your mind is a wise friend giving you advice based on everything it knows.

However, just like any machine, the mind sometimes feels overwhelmed or confused. It's essential to take care of it by giving it rest, doing things that make you happy, and talking about your feelings with someone you trust. This way, your mind can work better and help you live happier."

Mindset refers to a collection of beliefs, attitudes, assumptions, and mental frameworks that shape how individuals perceive the world, interpret situations, and respond to challenges. It is the lens through which people view themselves, others, and the world around them. Mindset significantly influences thoughts, behaviours, decisions, and overall outlook on life.

A mindset is just a series of beliefs and our beliefs are created by repeated thoughts.

Types of Mindset

Mixed Mindset and Growth Mindset

Fixed Mindset: People with a fixed mindset tend to believe that their abilities, intelligence, and talents are static and predetermined. They may think that they're born with a certain level of intelligence, skill, or talent and that these qualities cannot be significantly changed. Consequently, individuals with a fixed mindset may avoid challenges, feel threatened by the success of others, and see effort as fruitless since they believe they possess a limited set of skills and capacities.

For Example : Imagine you've just completed a project at work, and your manager provides you with feedback during a one-on-one meeting.

You receive the feedback and immediately think, "I can't believe my manager is criticizing my work. This is unfair. I'm just not good at this. I'll probably never improve, so why bother trying?"

In this example, a person with a fixed mindset reacts defensively to feedback, viewing it as a personal attack and believing that their abilities are static and unlikely to improve. This response may lead to a reluctance to seek further feedback or engage in efforts to enhance their skills.

2 Growth Mindset: Those with a growth mindset believe that abilities and intelligence can be developed through dedication, hard work, learning, and perseverance. They view challenges as opportunities to grow, embrace failures as learning experiences, and understand that effort and practice can lead to improvement and mastery in various areas of life. People with a growth mindset are more resilient, open to new experiences, and willing to take risks to expand their capabilities.

It's important to note that mindset is not a fixed, unchangeable trait. It can be developed, cultivated, and altered over time. Individuals can shift from a fixed mindset to a growth mindset by recognizing their beliefs and thought patterns and consciously working to adopt a more open and adaptive way of thinking.

Understanding and intentionally developing a growth-oriented mindset can lead to increased resilience, improved learning and adaptability, and a more positive approach to facing challenges and pursuing goals in various aspects of life.

Remember that It is our mind that makes us feel happy or unhappy. The big question to solve is the characteristics of being happy or sorrowful.

Let us understand in simple words through a small story the difference between Mixed Mindset and **Growth Mindset**

Once upon a time in a little town, there were two friends, Lily and Max. They both loved to draw and paint. They often entered art competitions at school.

Lily had a fixed mindset. She believed that people were either born talented artists or not. She thought that her artistic abilities were fixed and unchangeable. Whenever she encountered a difficult drawing or received constructive feedback, she felt discouraged. Lily thought, "I'm just not good at this, I'll never be as good as the others."

Max, on the other hand, had a different view. He had a growth mindset. He believed that he could improve his artistic skills with practice and effort. Whenever he faced a challenging drawing, he saw it as an opportunity to learn. He thought, even if he made mistakes, "I'll get better if I keep trying. I just need more practice."

One day, there was a drawing competition at their school. Lily and Max both decided to draw a picture of their town. Lily started to feel anxious and worried. She was scared that her drawing wouldn't be good enough. She rushed through her drawing and was unhappy with the result. When the judges reviewed her work and gave her some improvement tips, she felt upset and thought, "I'll never be as good as the others."

On the other hand, Max took his time and put in a lot of effort. He carefully drew every detail of the town. He felt excited when the judges reviewed his work and suggested improvements. He thought, "I can do even better next time!"

In the end, Max won the competition. Lily felt even more disheartened and thought, "I'll never be as good as him."

This story shows how a fixed mindset, like Lily's, can make someone feel stuck and discouraged when facing challenges. Meanwhile, a growth mindset, like Max's, can help someone see challenges as opportunities to learn and improve.

The story's moral is that having a fixed mindset might hold you back and make you feel like your abilities are set in stone. But having a growth mindset can help you see that you can improve at anything you put your mind to with effort and practice.

CHAPTER 2
PSYCHOLOGY OF MINDSET

Upbringing and Early Experiences: How we're raised, and our experiences in our early life play a big part. The things we're told, the way we're treated by our parents, teachers, and friends, and the situations we face when we're young all shape how we see the world and ourselves.

A) Early Childhood Environment: Consider two individuals, Emily and James, who had different experiences in their early family life that influenced their attitudes and beliefs about relationships.

Emily: Growing up, Emily witnessed her parents maintain a healthy and communicative relationship. They resolved conflicts through discussion, compromise, and understanding. Her family environment was supportive, nurturing, and emphasized the value of open communication, trust, and empathy.

James: In contrast, James grew up in a family where conflicts were often avoided or resolved through arguments and fights. His parents' relationship was tumultuous, characterized by frequent misunderstandings and ineffective communication. This environment made James perceive relationships as volatile and filled with conflict.

Impact on Mindset: As Emily and James navigate their own relationships as adults, their early experiences shape their attitudes and behaviors:

Emily has developed a positive attitude towards relationships. Her upbringing has instilled in her the importance of communication, trust, and empathy. She tends to approach relationships with a mindset focused on understanding, compromise, and healthy communication. She values these qualities and actively seeks to nurture and maintain healthy connections.

James, due to his early experiences, may have developed a negative attitude towards relationships. He might perceive conflict as a norm, struggle with trust issues, and find it challenging to communicate effectively in relationships. His past experiences might lead him to expect conflicts and misunderstandings, making it difficult for him to establish and maintain healthy connections.

Impact on Adulthood: These differing mindsets significantly influence their experiences in adult relationships:

Emily, with her positive attitude, is more likely to build and maintain healthy, fulfilling relationships. She navigates conflicts with maturity and seeks mutual understanding, fostering strong and supportive connections.

James, with his negative mindset, might face challenges in his relationships. He might find it hard to trust, communicate openly, and healthily handle conflicts. His past experiences might hinder the development of secure and harmonious relationships.

This example demonstrates how early life experiences surrounding relationships can profoundly influence one's mindset and attitudes towards establishing and maintaining healthy, fulfilling relationships in adulthood.

Cultural Influences: The culture we grow up in—its values, beliefs, and traditions—also impacts our mindset. Different cultures have different ways of thinking about success, failure, and personal growth, which affect how we see the world.

Cultural influence plays a pivotal role in shaping an individual's mindset. Here's an example that highlights how culture can impact mindset:

Example:

Cultural Context:

Consider two individuals, Maria and Ken, raised in different cultural environments, emphasising contrasting values regarding individualism and collectivism.

Maria:

Grew up in a culture that highly values collectivism. Her family, community, and social structures emphasize interdependence, cooperation, and the importance of group harmony. From an early age, Maria was taught to prioritize the community's and family's needs and goals over personal desires. Success is often seen as a collective achievement rather than an individual one.

Ken:

Comes from a culture that predominantly values individualism. In his upbringing, the focus is on personal achievement, independence, and self-reliance. The culture encourages standing out, pursuing personal goals, and expressing individual opinions and preferences. Success is often attributed to individual effort and talent.

Impact on Mindset:

As a result of their cultural backgrounds, Maria and Ken have developed differing mindsets:

Maria has a collective mindset. She values cooperation, harmony, and the interconnectedness of the community. Her sense of identity is strongly tied to her relationships and her group. She's more likely to prioritize the needs of her family or community over personal ambitions.

Ken, with an individualistic mindset, values personal autonomy, self-expression, and the pursuit of personal goals. He's more inclined to assert his individual preferences and strive for personal success, emphasizing his own achievements and aspirations.

Impact on Decision-Making:

These contrasting mindsets significantly influence their decision-making and behavior:

Maria might consider the impact of her decisions on her family or community, seeking consensus and harmony in her interactions. She's likely to prioritize the collective good over personal desires and is more comfortable with conformity and cooperation.

Ken may make decisions based on his personal ambitions and aspirations, valuing independence and autonomy. He's more inclined to prioritize his individual goals and preferences, even if they conflict with the expectations or desires of the group.

Impact on Society:

In broader society, these different mindsets can affect various aspects:

In the workplace, Maria might excel in team-oriented environments that require collaboration and consensus-building.

Ken might thrive in individualistic settings where personal achievement and standing out are valued.

This example illustrates how cultural influences related to values of individualism and collectivism shape one's mindset, influencing their priorities, decision-making, and interactions within society.

Education and Learning:

What we're taught and learn as we grow, both in and out of school, can shape our mindset. For instance, being encouraged to learn from mistakes or being praised for effort rather than just innate abilities can affect how we approach challenges.

Personal Experiences:

The things that happen to us as we grow up, such as successes, failures, and the way we deal with them, influence our mindset. These experiences can shape our beliefs about our abilities and the world around us.

Mindsets often stem from experiences, influences, and societal factors. For instance, a person's upbringing, education, and cultural background can significantly impact their mindset. Praise, feedback, and the way challenges are approached during formative years can contribute to the development of a particular mindset

Our mindset results from all these things coming together, creating how we see the world, how we approach challenges, and our beliefs about our abilities. It's a mix of our early life, our surroundings, and what we've learned.

Example:

Cultural Context:

Imagine two individuals, Priya and Miguel, raised in distinct cultural environments that shape their perspectives on time.

Priya: Hails from a culture that has a polychronic view of time. In her upbringing, time is perceived as flexible and less rigid. Relationships and interactions are valued over strict adherence to schedules. Punctuality might be less emphasized, and flexibility in timing is a norm, allowing for social connections to take precedence.

Miguel: Grew up in a culture that follows a monochronic view of time. In his environment, time is seen as linear, structured, and valued with a focus on punctuality and adhering to schedules. There is an emphasis on completing tasks within set timeframes, and being on time is highly regarded as a sign of respect.

Impact on Mindset:

As a result of their cultural backgrounds, Priya and Miguel have developed differing perceptions of time:

Priya has a more flexible view of time. She's accustomed to a less structured approach, prioritizing relationships and experiences over strictly following time schedules. Flexibility and adaptability in time management are more natural for her.

Miguel has a more structured approach to time. Punctuality and adhering to schedules are significant to him. He values the importance of timelines and sees them as essential for productivity and success.

Impact on Daily Life:

These contrasting views on time significantly affect their daily lives and interactions:

Priya might feel comfortable with flexible time management, being more relaxed about punctuality in social interactions and being flexible with scheduling.

Miguel may find it crucial to adhere to schedules, prioritize efficiency, and be on time for appointments or meetings. He might feel discomfort or frustration in situations where timing is more fluid.

Impact in Business or Professional Settings:

In business or professional environments, these differing time orientations can lead to various approaches:

Priya might excel in roles that require adaptability and flexibility in working hours, such as roles that involve multicultural communication or fluid deadlines.

Miguel might perform exceptionally in structured work environments with tight schedules and a strong emphasis on punctuality, such as corporate settings with strict timelines.

This example illustrates how cultural influences regarding perceptions of time orientation can significantly shape an individual's mindset and behaviors, including social interactions and professional environments.

Impact on Behavior:

Mindset plays a pivotal role in shaping behavior. A fixed mindset might hinder individuals from taking risks or pursuing challenges due to the fear of failure. On the other hand, a growth mindset can lead to more resilience, persistence, and an inclination to embrace challenges with enthusiasm.

Let's consider an example that demonstrates how an individual's mindset can influence their behavior in a specific situation:

Example:

Resilience in the Face of Adversity

Context: Meet two individuals, Sarah and Mark, both facing a similar challenge, such as the loss of a job.

Sarah: Has developed a resilient mindset through her life experiences. She views setbacks as opportunities for growth, believing that effort and perseverance can lead to success. Her past experiences have taught her that failures are a natural part of life and can serve as learning opportunities.

Mark: Approaches challenges with a fixed mindset. He believes that abilities are innate and that setbacks reflect personal inadequacy. Mark tends to avoid challenges where he might not excel immediately, and he's prone to viewing failures as a reflection of his capabilities.

Impact on Behavior:

Facing the loss of a job, both Sarah and Mark exhibit different behaviors based on their mindsets:

Sarah, with her resilient mindset, sees the job loss as a temporary setback. She immediately begins searching for new opportunities, learning from her previous job experiences, and using the situation as a chance to explore new career paths. She remains optimistic and is willing to put in the effort needed to bounce back.

Mark, with his fixed mindset, feels defeated by the job loss. He dwells on the idea that losing the job confirms his lack of ability. Mark may hesitate to actively seek new opportunities, feeling demotivated and worried about facing potential rejections. He might not readily consider the lessons from the experience and may struggle to see the setback as a chance for growth.

Outcome:

The difference in mindset leads to distinct outcomes for Sarah and Mark:

Sarah, with her resilient approach, eventually finds a new job that aligns better with her skills and interests. She views the experience as a learning curve, gaining new skills and insights along the way, ultimately bouncing back stronger from the setback.

Mark, with his fixed mindset, might struggle for a longer period to find new employment. His mindset creates obstacles in seeking new opportunities, which could result in a longer period of unemployment and potentially reinforce his belief in his lack of abilities.

This example illustrates how an individual's mindset, whether resilient or fixed, significantly influences their behavior when faced with challenges, subsequently impacting their ability to adapt and succeed in adverse situations.

Neuroplasticity and Mindset Change:

Understanding neuroplasticity, the brain's ability to reorganize itself and form new neural connections, is crucial in fostering a change in mindset. By adopting a growth mindset, individuals can rewire their brains to perceive challenges as opportunities for growth.

Neuroplasticity refers to the brain's ability to reorganize itself by forming new neural connections throughout life. This ability allows individuals to adapt, learn, and change their mindset. Here's an example illustrating neuroplasticity and mindset change:

Example:

Shifting from a Fixed Mindset to a Growth Mindset

Context:

Let's consider an individual named Emily who has typically exhibited a fixed mindset in various aspects of her life, believing that abilities are innate and static.

Emily: Grew up with the belief that intelligence and talent are predetermined traits. When faced with challenges, she often feels discouraged, assuming that her abilities are limited. This mindset hinders her from embracing new opportunities and persisting through difficulties.

Neuroplasticity and Mindset Change:

Emily becomes aware of the concept of a growth mindset, which suggests that abilities can be developed and improved through dedication and effort. She decides to actively work on shifting her fixed mindset to a growth mindset.

Practising New Thought Patterns:

Emily starts consciously challenging her own beliefs about abilities being fixed. She self-reflects, acknowledges her fixed mindset tendencies, and consciously reframes her thoughts. For instance, instead of believing her intelligence is a fixed trait, she begins to affirm that she can improve through learning and practice.

Embracing Challenges:

Emily deliberately seeks out challenges that she usually avoids due to her fixed mindset. She approaches them with the mindset that effort and learning can lead to improvement. When faced with difficulties, she consciously reminds herself that it's an opportunity for growth.

Reinforcing Positive Behaviors:

Emily consistently reinforces her efforts and the learning process, acknowledging her progress, no matter how small. This helps in rewiring her brain to adapt to the new growth-oriented mindset.

Neuroplasticity at Work:

As Emily actively works on transitioning her mindset from fixed to growth-oriented:

Over time, her brain begins to form new neural pathways that support the growth mindset. The brain's plasticity allows for the strengthening of connections associated with adaptability, learning, and resilience.

With consistent practice, Emily's brain rewires itself to reinforce the belief that abilities can be developed. As a result, she becomes more open to challenges, more resilient in the face of setbacks, and starts seeing failures as opportunities for learning.

This example demonstrates how individuals can leverage neuroplasticity to change their mindset actively. Through intentional effort, self-reflection, and a deliberate shift in thought patterns, Emily can rewire her brain and adopt a more growth-oriented perspective, thereby embracing challenges and opportunities for growth.

Application in Education, Business, and Personal Development:

Mindset psychology has practical applications in various fields. In education, it influences teaching methods and student motivation. In business, it impacts organizational culture, leadership, and innovation. In personal development, it guides individuals in setting and achieving goals.

Let's explore examples of how mindset can be applied in education, business, and personal development to highlight its impact in these areas:

Education

Mindset in the Classroom:

Growth Mindset Teaching Approach:

Educators embrace a growth mindset philosophy, encouraging students to believe in their capacity to learn and develop skills. They provide feedback emphasising effort, perseverance, and learning from mistakes rather than solely focusing on grades or innate abilities.

Resilience and Learning:

Students are taught to view challenges as opportunities for growth. They're encouraged to persist through difficulties, fostering resilience and a love for learning. This mindset shift allows students to approach education with a positive attitude toward effort and improvement.

Business

Mindset in the Workplace:

Innovation and Adaptability:

Companies foster a culture that values a growth mindset, encouraging employees to embrace innovation and adaptability. Employees are encouraged to take calculated risks, learn from failures, and continuously develop new skills and knowledge.

Leadership Development:

Business leaders adopt a growth mindset, promoting a culture where learning and improvement are central. They prioritize mentorship, feedback, and continuous learning, encouraging their teams to explore new ideas and approaches.

Personal Development

Mindset in Personal Growth:

Self-Improvement and Resilience:

Individuals focus on personal development by adopting a growth mindset. They acknowledge that abilities can be developed through dedication and hard work. This allows them to approach challenges with resilience, viewing setbacks as opportunities for growth.

Embracing Change:

Those pursuing personal development understand that mindset influences outcomes. They work on shifting from fixed to growth-oriented thinking, allowing them to adapt to change, take on challenges, and pursue continuous self-improvement.

Overarching Impact

In all these areas, the application of mindset plays a crucial role in shaping behaviors and outcomes:

In education, it promotes a love for learning and resilience in students.

It encourages innovation, adaptability, and continuous improvement within organizations.

In personal development, it fosters a more resilient and adaptable approach to life's challenges and opportunities.

Applying a growth mindset across these domains enhances learning, encourages a proactive approach to challenges, and fosters a culture of continuous improvement and development. As individuals and organizations shift their mindset from fixed to growth-oriented, it leads to improved outcomes, greater adaptability, and a positive attitude towards learning and development.

Cultivating a Growth Mindset:

Strategies such as embracing challenges, persisting in the face of setbacks, seeking learning opportunities, and viewing effort as a path to mastery can help in cultivating a growth mindset.

Cultivating a growth mindset involves believing that abilities and intelligence can be developed through dedication and hard work. Here's an example demonstrating how an individual might actively cultivate a growth mindset:

Example:

Emily's Journey to Cultivate a Growth Mindset

Background:

Emily, a college student, has noticed she often shies away from challenges and feels discouraged by setbacks. She wants to change her approach and adopt a growth mindset to improve her learning experience and personal development.

Steps in Cultivating a Growth Mindset:

Self-Reflection and Awareness:

Emily begins by reflecting on her own fixed mindset tendencies. She recognizes that she tends to believe abilities are fixed and struggles with challenges.

Embracing Challenges: She actively seeks new challenges in her coursework, deliberately choosing tasks that push her out of her comfort zone. When faced with difficulties, she consciously reminds herself that effort and learning are keys to improvement.

Changing Self-Talk and Beliefs:

Emily consciously adjusts her self-talk. Instead of saying, "I'm not good at this," she reframes it to, "I can improve with practice and effort." This change in language helps alter her beliefs about her abilities.

Learning from Setbacks:

She reframes failures as learning opportunities. Emily makes it a point to analyze what went wrong and what she can learn from these experiences, rather than seeing setbacks as a reflection of her intelligence.

Seeking Feedback and Growth Opportunities:

Emily actively seeks feedback from professors and peers, viewing it as a chance for improvement. She participates in study groups and engages in discussions to learn from different perspectives.

Persistence and Effort:

She consistently puts in effort, recognizing that learning and skill development require dedication and perseverance. Emily sets goals and works steadily towards achieving them, celebrating the progress made along the way.

Celebrating Progress and Growth:

Finally, Emily acknowledges and celebrates her progress, no matter how small. She recognizes her improvement, reinforcing the idea that effort leads to growth.

Outcomes:

As Emily actively cultivates a growth mindset:

She becomes more resilient in the face of challenges and setbacks.

Her learning experience improves as she starts embracing challenges and persisting through difficulties.

Emily's confidence grows as she sees her efforts translating into tangible improvements in her abilities and understanding.

This example demonstrates how an individual, like Emily, can actively cultivate a growth mindset through deliberate actions, self-reflection, and a conscious shift in beliefs and behaviors. Over time, this shift fosters a more positive and growth-oriented approach to learning and personal development.

Peer Influence:

The friends and people we spend time with also impact our mindset. The opinions and behaviors of our friends can shape our thinking and our approach to various situations.

Peer influence can significantly impact an individual's mindset. Here's an example illustrating how peers can influence mindset:

Example

Peer Influence on Academic Mindset Context:

Consider a group of high school students: Sarah, Mark, and John.

Sarah has a growth mindset, believing that intelligence can be developed through effort and learning.

Mark has a fixed mindset, thinking that intelligence is largely fixed and innate.

John is unsure about his beliefs but is easily influenced by his peers' perspectives.

Influence of Peers:

Positive Influence (Sarah on John):

Sarah consistently demonstrates a growth mindset. She openly discusses the benefits of hard work and the idea that intelligence can be developed over time. John, being easily influenced, starts to adopt some of Sarah's views. He becomes more open to the concept of a growth mindset.

Negative Influence (Mark on John):

Mark consistently expresses his fixed mindset beliefs, often stating that intelligence is predetermined and unchangeable. John, influenced by Mark's perspective, starts to doubt the idea of a growth mindset. He begins to lean more towards the belief that abilities are fixed and innate.

Outcome:

John's beliefs about intelligence and abilities start shifting under his peers' influence.

While he is inclined to adopt a growth mindset due to Sarah's influence, Mark's consistent promotion of a fixed mindset creates conflict and confusion within John's beliefs.

Impact on Behavior and Performance:

John, affected by the differing mindsets of his peers, starts to demonstrate a mix of attitudes. He may exhibit a willingness to work hard and improve (from Sarah's influence) but might also doubt his potential for growth due to the fixed mindset influence from Mark.

Conclusion:

This example illustrates how peer influence can significantly impact an individual's mindset. The conflicting mindsets of peers can create a challenging environment for someone like John, causing uncertainty and confusion about their own beliefs. It shows that peer influence plays a vital role in shaping an individual's mindset, especially during formative stages, and highlights the importance of positive influences in nurturing a growth-oriented perspective.

Explaining the psychology of mindset involves understanding how one's beliefs about abilities and intelligence shape behavior, perception, and ultimately, the course of one's life. It's about recognizing the power of our thoughts and attitudes in influencing our potential for growth, success, and well-being.

CHAPTER 3
HUMAN EMOTIONS THAT INFLUENCE OUR MIND

Human emotions are diverse and can significantly impact our mind and overall well-being. Some key emotions that have a substantial effect on our mental state include:

Happiness

Happiness is a complex and subjective emotional and mental state characterized by feelings of joy, contentment, satisfaction, and well-being. It is a state of mind that is often influenced by a variety of factors, including individual temperament, life circumstances, relationships, health, and personal fulfillment. Feeling joy, contentment, and satisfaction can positively impact our mind by enhancing mood, motivation, and overall mental health. There are different sources through which we feel happy. For instance :

Joy from Achieving Goals:

Imagine the happiness you feel when you've been working hard on something, like completing a puzzle or scoring well in a test. The feeling of accomplishment and satisfaction is happiness.

Let us see its effects on our mindset:-

Let's imagine you set a goal for yourself, like saving money to buy a new smartphone. You work hard, save a little money each month, and finally, you have enough to purchase that phone. When you achieve this goal and hold that new smartphone in your hands, a feeling of joy and accomplishment rushes through you.

Now, think about the effects of this joy on your mind. First of all, you feel happy and satisfied because you set out to do something, and you did it! This sense of achievement makes your mind feel good about itself.

Secondly, achieving a goal often brings a boost of confidence. You proved to yourself that you are capable of reaching targets you set. This confidence can spill over into other areas of your life, making you feel more positive and capable in general.

Moreover, the joy from achieving a goal can also reduce stress. The process of working towards something, facing challenges, and finally succeeding can be a bit stressful at times. However, when you reach that goal, all that stress tends to fade away, leaving you with a sense of relief and peace of mind.

In simple terms, the joy from achieving goals is like a mental reward. It makes you feel happy, confident, and less stressed. It's like a pat on the back from your own mind, telling you, "Hey, you did it, and you can do even more!" This positive feeling can motivate you to tackle new challenges and set even bigger goals in the future.

Spending Time with Loved Ones:

Think of moments spent with family and friends, laughing, sharing stories, or celebrating special occasions. The warmth and joy you feel in those moments represent happiness.

Let's dive into the story of Ravi, a common man in an Indian village, to understand the effects of spending time with loved ones on our mindset.

Ravi, a hardworking farmer, often found himself caught up in the challenges of tending to his fields and providing for his family. One day, after a particularly demanding week, he decided to take a break and spend quality time with his loved ones.

He gathered his family – his wife, children, and parents – and they decided to have a simple picnic by the river near their village. The atmosphere was relaxed, with the sound of flowing water and the warmth of the sun creating a serene setting.

As they shared a meal and engaged in light-hearted conversations, Ravi felt a remarkable shift in his mindset. The worries of the farm and daily struggles seemed to fade away, replaced by a deep sense of contentment and joy. The laughter of his children and the comforting presence of his family created a positive and uplifting atmosphere.

In this moment, Ravi experienced the powerful effects of spending time with loved ones. The stresses that had burdened his mind were temporarily set aside, and a newfound appreciation for the simple joys of life emerged. The bonds strengthened during this time filled him with a sense of belonging and support.

As the sun set, Ravi returned home with a refreshed mindset. The challenges hadn't disappeared, but his ability to face them had been rejuvenated by the love and connection he shared with his family. The positive effects lingered, influencing his interactions with others in the village and enhancing his overall well-being.

This story illustrates that spending time with loved ones acts as a mental and emotional recharge. It provides a sanctuary from life's pressures, fostering a positive mindset and reinforcing the importance of relationships in navigating life's journey. In the heart of these connections, individuals like Ravi find strength, joy, and a renewed perspective on the challenges they face.

Feeling pleasure in small matters

In our daily life we unknowingly do some such acts which look small but have big impact. Normally we do not pay careful attention to these matters . But these small acts impact our mindset in a unique way.

Let me share a simple story to explain the impact of finding pleasure in small matters on our mindset.

Meet Anil, a shopkeeper in a bustling Indian market. Anil had a small stationery shop, and his days were filled with the usual challenges of running a business. One day, as he was organizing his shelves, he noticed a little girl entering his shop with wide-eyed curiosity.

The girl approached a display of colorful pens and notebooks, her eyes sparkling with excitement. Anil, seeing her enthusiasm, decided to gift her a small notebook and a set of vibrant pens. The joy on the girl's face was priceless.

From that day on, Anil started finding pleasure in small matters. He began to notice the beauty in everyday moments—whether it was the laughter of children playing outside his shop or the vibrant colors of the sunset.

As Anil focused on these small, joyful experiences, he realized that his mindset began to shift. The pressures of running a business didn't weigh as heavily on him. He found moments of delight in helping customers, chatting with neighbors, and appreciating the simple joys around him.

Anil's story illustrates the impact of finding pleasure in small matters on our mindset. By taking the time to appreciate and enjoy little moments, he not only brought positivity into his own life but also created a more welcoming and cheerful atmosphere in his shop. The ripple effect extended to his customers and the community, creating a more uplifting and enjoyable environment for everyone.

In essence, the story suggests that finding pleasure in small matters can act as a powerful tool to cultivate a positive mindset. It's like sprinkling a bit of joy on the ordinary aspects of life, making the journey more delightful and the challenges more manageable.

Sadness:

Sadness can affect our mind by causing feelings of loss, disappointment, or grief. It may lead to lower energy levels and a sense of withdrawal. Loss or Grief: When you experience the loss of a loved one, a pet, or something important to you, it can bring deep sadness. The feeling of emptiness or sorrow associated with that loss is sadness.

Sadness is a complex and multifaceted emotional experience characterized by feelings of sorrow, unhappiness, or grief. It is a natural and universal human emotion that can arise in response to various situations, such as loss, disappointment, or unmet expectations. Sadness often involves a sense of heaviness, a lowering of mood, and a temporary decrease in overall well-being.

Let us discuss few of sad emotions effecting our mindset.

Disappointment:

Let's delve into the story of Arjun, a common man in an Indian town, to understand the effects of disappointment on our mindset.

Arjun had been preparing for a government job exam for months. He had invested time, energy, and hope into this pursuit, envisioning a more stable future for himself and his family. The day of the exam arrived with a mix of nerves and anticipation.

After the long and challenging exam, Arjun felt a sense of relief, believing he had performed well. However, when the results were announced, he was shocked to find out that he had not qualified. The disappointment hit him hard, and a wave of sadness and frustration washed over him.

As Arjun grappled with the news, he noticed a change in his mindset. The initial excitement and confidence were replaced by self-doubt and a feeling of failure. Thoughts like, "Did I not study hard enough?" or "What will I tell my family?" started to dominate his thinking.

The disappointment not only affected Arjun's perception of his abilities but also influenced his interactions with those around him. He became withdrawn, avoiding discussions about the exam or his future plans. The enthusiasm he once had for learning and improvement dwindled, and a cloud of gloom settled over his usual optimistic demeanor.

However, as time passed, Arjun began to reflect on the disappointment. He realized that setbacks are a part of life and don't define one's worth or potential. Slowly, he started picking up the pieces and channeling his disappointment into renewed determination. Arjun decided to learn from the experience, identify areas for improvement, and give the exam another shot.

In the end, Arjun's story illustrates that disappointment can have a profound impact on our mindset. Initially, it may lead to self-doubt, sadness, and a negative outlook. However, with resilience and a shift in perspective, disappointment can also become a stepping stone for personal growth and renewed determination. It's a reminder that setbacks are not the end but rather an opportunity to reassess, learn, and move forward.

Imagine when something you were looking forward to doesn't happen, like missing out on a special event or not getting something you really wanted. The feeling of letdown or dissatisfaction is a form of sadness.

Loneliness:

Feeling alone or disconnected from others can bring about sadness. This could occur when you're missing someone, feeling isolated, or longing for companionship. It's the feeling of emptiness or longing for connection.

Let's explore the impact of loneliness on our mindset through the story of Aarav, a young man living in a bustling Indian city.

Aarav, an ambitious and hardworking youth, moved to the city to pursue his dreams of a successful career. He secured a job in a big company, but the fast-paced city life often left him feeling isolated. Despite being surrounded by people, he struggled to form deep connections and found himself grappling with a sense of loneliness.

His work hours were long, and the demands of the city were relentless. Aarav's weekends were often spent alone in his apartment. The initial excitement of city life began to fade, and a feeling of isolation crept into his daily routine.

As loneliness settled in, Aarav noticed changes in his mindset. He became more introspective, dwelling on negative thoughts about not having a strong support system. The absence of meaningful social interactions began to affect his confidence and overall well-being. The once vibrant and optimistic Aarav felt a growing sense of sadness and disconnection.

One day, Aarav decided to attend a local community event. It was there that he met people who shared similar interests and aspirations. Slowly, he started building connections and forming friendships. The impact on his mindset was profound. The loneliness that had cast a shadow over his thoughts began to lift, replaced by a sense of belonging and support.

As Aarav became more socially engaged, his mindset underwent a positive transformation. The friendships he cultivated provided a support system that helped him navigate the challenges of city life. The loneliness that once weighed heavily on his mind gradually dissipated, making room for a more optimistic and fulfilled outlook.

Aarav's story underscores the impact of loneliness on our mindset. It can lead to feelings of sadness, isolation, and a negative perception of oneself. However, by actively seeking social connections and fostering relationships, individuals like Aarav can experience a positive shift in their mindset. Loneliness may persist, but meaningful connections have the power to alleviate its effects and contribute to a more positive and resilient mental state.

Both happiness and sadness are common human emotions. Happiness brings feelings of joy, contentment, and fulfillment, while sadness brings feelings of sorrow, disappointment, or a sense of loss. Emotions are a natural part of being human and experiencing the highs and lows of life.

Having trouble at home

In a small town in India, the Verma family was known for their illustrious lineage and respected standing in the community. Mr. Verma, the patriarch, had upheld the family's honor with great pride. However, as the years passed, disagreements and clashes among family members began to erode the once-strong foundation of the Verma household.

The source of the conflict was rooted in differing opinions and contrasting personalities. The once-close siblings found themselves entangled in disputes over the family business, traditions, and even the direction in which the family should progress. The atmosphere at home, once filled with warmth and laughter, became strained and fraught with tension.

Mr. Verma, torn between loyalty to his children and a desire for familial harmony, found himself in the middle of the familial storm. Mrs. Verma, the matriarch, tried to mediate, but the chasms seemed to widen. The family, once a symbol of unity, now faced a crisis that threatened to tear them apart.

As the clashes among family members escalated, the Verma household became a battleground of emotions. Resentment and misunderstandings festered, casting a dark cloud over the once-joyful home. The impact of the troubles at home began to seep into the minds and hearts of each family member.

Realizing the gravity of the situation, the Verma family took a step back. In a moment of reflection, they recognized that the strength of their family lay in their shared history and the love that had always bound them together. With a collective decision to prioritize reconciliation over discord, they initiated open and honest conversations.

Through heartfelt dialogues, the family members began to understand each other's perspectives. They acknowledged that differences were inevitable but could be navigated with respect and compromise. Slowly but steadily, the wounds of the past began to heal, and the family started rebuilding the bridges that had been damaged.

The impact of the clashes among family members, though tumultuous, became a catalyst for positive change. The Verma family emerged from the storm stronger, with a newfound appreciation for the importance of communication, empathy, and compromise in maintaining familial bonds. The troubles at home, once threatening to dismantle the family, ultimately became a transformative chapter that led to a more resilient and united Verma household.

Being ill, or caring for someone who is ill

In a bustling city in India, there lived the Mehta family. Mr. Mehta, the head of the household, was a hardworking software engineer, while Mrs. Mehta took care of the home and their two children, Aarav and Naina. The Mehtas were a close-knit family, and their modest apartment was filled with laughter and warmth.

One day, Mr. Mehta fell seriously ill. What started as a seemingly ordinary fever escalated into a more complicated health issue. The sudden change in their lives brought an air of anxiety to the once-vibrant Mehta household. Mrs. Mehta, a pillar of strength, took on the responsibility of caring for her ailing husband while still managing the daily needs of the family.

The Mehta children, Aarav and Naina, felt the shift in their home dynamics. Their once energetic father was now confined to bed, and the lively atmosphere they were accustomed to became more subdued. Mrs. Mehta juggled between her caregiving duties, running the household, and managing the emotional well-being of her children.

The extended family and neighbors, deeply rooted in the cultural values of support and community, rallied around the Mehta family. Aunties from the neighboring apartments took turns cooking meals, uncles assisted with household chores, and friends took the children out to ease their minds during this challenging time.

Aarav, being the older sibling, started to help his mother with small tasks around the house. Naina, though initially confused and worried, found solace in the presence of her supportive school friends and the community around her. The Mehtas, despite the adversity, were enveloped in a cocoon of care and concern that the community provided.

As Mr. Mehta gradually recovered, the Mehta family realized the power of collective empathy and support. The experience not only brought the family members closer but also strengthened the bonds with their neighbors and friends. The mindset around illness in the Indian scenario, as portrayed in this story, emphasizes the importance of community and the collective effort to navigate through difficult times.

In the face of illness, the support from the extended community becomes a crucial aspect of the healing process. The story of the Mehta family reflects the resilience and compassion inherent in Indian society, where caring for someone who is ill is considered a shared responsibility, bringing not just physical recovery but emotional healing as well.

Changes in thoughts

In a remote village in India, there lived a man named Ravi. Ravi was known for his traditional values and conservative mindset. He had grown up with certain beliefs passed down through generations, shaping his perspectives on various aspects of life.

One day, a group of young, educated individuals from the city visited the village. They organized a community event to discuss the importance of education for all, breaking away from some of the traditional norms that had long governed the village. Ravi, initially skeptical and resistant to change, attended the event out of curiosity.

As he listened to the speakers passionately talk about the transformative power of education, Ravi felt a gradual shift in his thoughts. The stories of individuals who had overcome adversity through education resonated with him. He began to question some of the beliefs he had held onto for years, particularly those that limited the educational opportunities for certain members of the community.

In the weeks that followed, Ravi started interacting with the young organizers and participating in discussions about the positive impact of change. He realized that embracing new ideas did not mean abandoning tradition entirely; rather, it meant evolving with the times while preserving the core values that mattered most.

Ravi's changing thoughts had a ripple effect on his interactions within the village. He started encouraging young children, including his own grandchildren, to pursue education and dream beyond the conventional roles assigned by societal norms. This shift in mindset transformed not only Ravi's life but also the lives of those around him.

Over time, the village witnessed a positive change in its educational landscape. More children, irrespective of gender or caste, began attending school. The community started to understand the importance of adapting to new ideas without losing touch with their cultural roots.

Ravi's story reflects the profound impact a change in thought can have on one's mindset. In this Indian context, where cultural values often play a significant role, it highlights the potential for positive transformation when individuals are open to reconsidering long-held beliefs. The story also underscores the idea that evolving one's mindset can contribute to the progress and well-being of the entire community.

ANGER

This emotion can impact our mind by creating feelings of frustration, irritation, or even rage. It might lead to impulsivity and difficulty in reasoning or problem-solving.

Frustration from Unmet Expectations:

Consider a situation where you were expecting something to happen, but it didn't turn out as planned. The resulting feeling of irritation, annoyance, or frustration is a form of anger.

Let's imagine you're really looking forward to a fun day at the beach. You expect clear skies, warm sun, and a perfect day to relax. However, when you get there, it starts raining heavily. Now, imagine how disappointed and annoyed you would feel because what you expected didn't match reality. This feeling of disappointment and annoyance is similar to frustration from unmet expectations.

In simple words, frustration from unmet expectations is when things don't go the way you hoped or planned, and it makes you feel upset or irritated. It's like having a picture in your mind of how things should be, and when reality doesn't match that picture, it can be really frustrating.

Feeling Provoked or Offended:

Imagine someone says or does something that upsets or offends you. The intense emotional reaction, often accompanied by a desire to react or retaliate, is a manifestation of anger.

Let's imagine you're talking with a friend, and suddenly he says something that really hurts your feelings. It's like he stepped on your emotional toes. Feeling provoked or offended is a bit like that - it's when something someone says or does makes you feel upset, irritated, or hurt. It's like a little emotional jab that makes you react with strong emotions because what happened goes against what you find acceptable or respectful. So, feeling provoked or offended is basically when someone or something pushes your emotional buttons in a way that makes you feel upset or bothered.

Rage from Injustice:

Witnessing or experiencing something unfair or unjust might trigger a deeper form of anger, leading to a feeling of intense anger or outrage. For instance, seeing someone treated unfairly or witnessing an unfair decision could provoke such a reaction.

For example Imagine you're working in an office, and there's a clear policy about promotions based on performance. Now, if you consistently outperform your colleagues, but someone who hasn't done as well gets promoted instead, you might feel a sense of rage from injustice. It's that intense frustration and anger because you believe the promotion decision is unfair and doesn't align with the established rules or meritocracy in the workplace. In this scenario, the perceived injustice in the promotion process triggers a strong emotional response, akin to rage from injustice in an office setting.

FEAR :

Fear can significantly impact the mind by causing anxiety, worry, and stress. It might lead to a fight-or-flight response, affecting decision-making and overall mental clarity

Phobia or Specific Fear:

Consider someone who has an intense fear of heights (acrophobia) or spiders (arachnophobia). When faced with the feared object or situation, the feeling of panic, anxiety, or dread represents fear.

For example ;

Let's imagine you have a friend named Sam who is terrified of spiders. Every time Sam sees a spider, even a tiny one, he gets extremely scared. This fear of spiders is like a big, dark cloud hanging over Sam's thoughts. It affects how Sam feels and acts.

Now, think about how this fear might impact Sam's mindset. For one, Sam might constantly worry about the possibility of encountering a spider. The fear might also make Sam avoid certain places or activities where spiders could be present. So, the fear of spiders is not just about being scared in the moment; it influences how Sam thinks, what Sam does, and even where Sam goes.

In simple words, a phobia or specific fear can cast a shadow over someone's thoughts and actions, making them feel uneasy or anxious in situations related to their fear. It's like a powerful force that shapes the way they see and navigate the world around them.

Feeling Threatened:

Imagine being in a situation where you feel physically or emotionally threatened, such as being in a dark alley alone or encountering a wild animal. The overwhelming sense of danger or apprehension is fear.

For Example :

Let's imagine your friend, Sarah, is walking home alone at night, and suddenly she hears footsteps behind her. In that moment, she starts feeling threatened, like there might be danger. This feeling of being threatened is like a dark cloud that comes over her thoughts and influences how she feels and acts.

Now, think about how this feeling might impact Sarah's mindset. First off, she might become really alert and cautious, looking around to figure out where the footsteps are coming from. She might start thinking about ways to stay safe, like walking faster or taking a different route. This feeling of being threatened doesn't just make her scared in that moment; it affects how she sees the situation and makes decisions to protect herself.

In simple words, when you feel threatened, it's like a strong force that changes how you think and what you do. You become more alert, cautious, and focused on staying safe. It's not just about feeling scared right then; it's about how this feeling shapes your mindset and actions to deal with the perceived threat.

Anxiety about the Future:

Fear can also manifest as worry about potential dangers or negative outcomes. For instance, worrying about failing an important exam or facing an uncertain future can lead to feelings of fear or anxiety.

For example ;

Let's imagine your friend, Alex, has this constant worry about what's going to happen in the future. It's like a cloud of anxiety hanging over Alex's thoughts. This anxiety about the future affects how Alex feels and acts.

Think about it this way:

Alex might be always thinking about what might go wrong, what challenges might come up, and if things will work out okay. This worry doesn't just stay in the background; it's there when Alex is making decisions or planning things. It's like a heavy feeling that influences how Alex sees the future.

In simple words, when you're anxious about the future, it's like having a lot of worries and uncertainties on your mind. It can make you feel uneasy and affect how you approach things, even before they happen. It's not just about feeling anxious; it's about how this anxiety shapes your mindset and reactions as you think about what's to come.

Both anger and fear are natural human emotions. Anger usually emerges in response to frustration or feeling provoked, while fear arises as a response to perceived threats or danger. Understanding and managing these emotions is important for maintaining emotional well-being and healthy responses to various situations.

Surprise :

A sudden, unexpected event or news can trigger surprise. It can impact our mind by momentarily altering our emotional state and reactions.

Unexpected Gift or Gesture:

Imagine receiving a surprise gift from someone unexpectedly. The sudden feeling of joy or amazement at the unexpected act is an example of surprise.

For example:

Imagine your friend, Lily, is having a regular day when, out of the blue, someone gives her a surprise gift or a thoughtful gesture, like a nice compliment or a helping hand. It's like a burst of happiness that suddenly lights up her day.

Now, think about how this unexpected gift or gesture might impact Lily's mindset. First off, she might feel really happy and appreciated. This positive experience can make her day much better. It could also make her feel more positive about herself and the people around her. So, it's not just about the gift itself; it's about how it can lift Lily's mood and make her see things in a brighter and more positive way.

In simple words, when someone does something unexpectedly nice for you, like giving a gift or a kind gesture, it's like a little boost of joy. It makes you feel happier, more appreciated, and can even change how you view the world around you. It's like a positive spark that brightens up your thoughts and feelings.

Sudden News or Announcement:

Consider getting unexpected news, such as learning about a surprise party being planned for you or receiving sudden positive or negative information. The feeling of sudden astonishment or disbelief is a form of surprise.

Let's say your friend, Jake, is going through a regular day when he suddenly hears some surprising news or a big announcement. It's like a shock that suddenly jumps into his thoughts and can affect how he feels and thinks.

Think about it this way:

If the news is good, like a surprise party being planned for Jake, it might make him really happy and excited. On the other hand, if it's unexpected bad news, like a sudden change at work, it might make him feel worried or stressed.

So, in simple words, when there's sudden news or an unexpected announcement, it's like a big wave of surprise that can change how you feel. It might bring joy if it's good news or worry if it's not-so-good news. Either way, it has a quick impact on your thoughts and emotions.

Unexpected Encounter:

Meeting someone unexpectedly or unexpectedly running into an old friend in an unexpected place can result in feelings of surprise. The suddenness and unplanned nature of the encounter can lead to surprise.

Let's imagine your friend, Maya, is walking in the park, and suddenly she bumps into someone she hasn't seen in years, like an old friend from school. This unexpected encounter is like a surprise that pops into her day and can change how she feels and thinks.

Think about it this way:

If Maya is happy to see her old friend, it might make her day much better. She could feel excited and nostalgic, remembering good times. On the other hand, if the encounter is with someone she'd rather not see, it might make her feel awkward or uneasy.

So, in simple words, when you have an unexpected encounter, it's like a sudden twist in your day that can bring joy, surprise, or maybe a bit of discomfort. It has a quick impact on your thoughts and emotions, changing how you feel in that moment.

Disgust:

This emotion can impact the mind by creating a strong aversion or repulsion towards something. It might lead to avoidance behavior and negative emotional responses.

Disgust is an emotion that can strongly influence our mindset. When we feel disgusted, our minds react with a strong aversion or repulsion toward something unpleasant or offensive.

This emotion can shape our thoughts, feelings, and behaviors in various ways:

Avoidance:

Disgust often leads to a desire to avoid the source of the feeling. For example, if we find a certain food disgusting, we are likely to avoid eating it.

Moral Judgment:

Disgust is not only related to physical things but can also be tied to moral or social issues. It can influence our judgment of others' behavior, making us more critical or judgmental.

Decision Making:

Disgust can impact our decision-making process. We might be inclined to reject certain options or choices that evoke feelings of disgust.

Memory:

Events or experiences associated with disgust can leave a lasting impact on our memory. We are more likely to remember things that elicit strong emotions, including disgust.

Social Interactions:

Disgust plays a role in social interactions by influencing our preferences for certain individuals or groups. It can affect who we choose to associate with and who we might distance ourselves from.

Reaction to Filth or Contamination:

Seeing something extremely dirty or contaminated can trigger feelings of disgust. The strong feeling of repulsion or wanting to distance oneself from the unclean object is an example of disgust.

Surprise and disgust are part of the wide range of human emotions. Surprise typically arises from sudden, unexpected events or situations, while disgust emerges in response to extremely unpleasant, offensive, or repulsive stimuli. Both emotions serve as natural responses to different stimuli and situations.

In simple terms, disgust serves as a powerful signal that guides our behavior, helping us navigate our environment by steering us away from things that might be harmful or undesirable

Love/Affection:

Feelings of love and affection can impact our mind positively by promoting bonding, trust, and a sense of well-being .Love or Affection has many forms like :-

Parental Love:

The deep and unconditional love that parents have for their children. This love is evident in the care, support, and nurturing parents provide, as well as the emotional bond and protective instincts they feel for their kids.

Romantic Love:

The affection and intense emotional connection between partners in a romantic relationship. It's displayed through acts of kindness, support, trust, and the desire to spend time together, showing care and consideration for each other.

Love for Friends:

The strong emotional bond and care between friends. It's seen in the support, loyalty, and understanding friends have for each other. They share experiences, listen to each other, and are there in times of need.

Love for Family:

The deep affection and bond between family members. This love is demonstrated through spending time together, supporting each other through challenges, and showing care and concern for the well-being of family members.

Love for Pets:

The strong attachment, care, and affection people feel for their pets. It's shown through the care, attention, and companionship they provide to their pets, considering them as part of the family.

Love and affection are fundamental emotions that create connections, strengthen relationships, and provide a sense of belonging and support in various contexts of life. These emotions are expressed through care, understanding, support, and a deep emotional connection with others.

Love and affection have profound impacts on our mindset, shaping our thoughts, emotions, and behaviors in positive ways. Here are some simple explanations of how love and affection influence our mindset:

Happiness and Well-being:

When we experience love and affection, our brains release feel-good chemicals like oxytocin, contributing to feelings of happiness and overall well-being. This positive emotional state can influence our mindset by fostering a more optimistic and content outlook on life.

Stress Reduction:

Love and affection can act as natural stress reducers. The emotional support we receive from loved ones can help lower stress levels, promoting a calmer and more relaxed mindset.

Increased Empathy:

Feeling loved and cared for can enhance our capacity for empathy. This means we may become more understanding and considerate of others, creating a positive mindset that values connection and compassion.

Boosted Self-Esteem:

Love and affection provide a sense of validation and acceptance. When we feel loved, we are more likely to develop a positive self-image, leading to greater self-esteem and confidence.

Motivation and Resilience:

Knowing that we are loved can serve as a powerful motivator. It gives us a sense of purpose and support, making us more resilient in the face of challenges. This positive mindset can fuel determination and the belief that we can overcome obstacles.

In simple terms, love and affection act as emotional nourishment for our minds, contributing to a more positive, resilient, and emotionally balanced mindset. They provide a foundation for personal growth, happiness, and fulfilling relationships.

Guilt/Shame :

These emotions can impact the mind negatively, leading to feelings of remorse, self-blame, or a sense of unworthiness.

After Making a Mistake:

Feeling guilt after making a mistake that affects someone else, such as accidentally breaking a friend's item or forgetting an important commitment.

Hurting Someone's Feelings:

Feeling guilty for saying something that unintentionally hurt someone's feelings or caused them distress.

Breaking a Promise:

Experiencing guilt when not fulfilling a promise made to someone, such as not showing up to an event after committing to attend.

Guilt and shame are emotions that can strongly affect our mindset, influencing how we think and feel about ourselves.

Here's a simple explanation of their impact:

Guilt:

When we feel guilty, it's like our mind telling us that we've done something wrong. This emotion prompts us to reflect on our actions and can push us to make amends or change our behavior. Guilt can make us more aware of our values and encourage us to take responsibility for our actions.

Shame:

Unlike guilt, which focuses on our actions, shame is more about feeling that there's something inherently wrong with us. It's a deep sense of embarrassment or unworthiness. Shame can be more intense and may lead to negative thoughts about ourselves, affecting our self-esteem and how we view our place in the world.

Motivation for Change:

Both guilt and shame can motivate us to make positive changes in our behavior. Guilt may encourage us to make amends and do better, while shame might drive us to seek personal growth and self-improvement to overcome negative feelings about ourselves.

Negative Thought Patterns:

Guilt and shame can lead to negative thought patterns. We might dwell on our mistakes or flaws, impacting our self-perception and creating a mindset that focuses on shortcomings rather than strengths.

Social Withdrawal:

Feeling guilty or ashamed can make us want to withdraw from social interactions. We may fear judgment from others and isolate ourselves, impacting our relationships and sense of connection with others.

In simple terms, guilt and shame act as signals that something needs attention or change. While guilt can guide us to correct our actions, shame may require a deeper exploration of our self-worth. It's important to address these emotions positively, using them as opportunities for personal growth rather than allowing them to create a negative and self-critical mindset.

Excitement:

Excitement can impact our mind by creating a surge of positive energy, anticipation, and enthusiasm.

Anticipation of a Special Event:

The feeling of excitement before a highly anticipated event, such as a birthday party, a concert of a favorite band, or an upcoming vacation, where the anticipation of the experience generates an excited feeling.

Receiving Positive News:

The emotion of excitement when receiving positive news, such as getting accepted into a dream college, receiving a job offer, or hearing about a promotion at work.

Accomplishment of a Goal:

Feeling excited upon achieving a personal goal or milestone, like completing a project, winning a competition, or accomplishing a difficult task.

Exploration of Something New:

The feeling of excitement when exploring or trying something new, like starting a new hobby, visiting a new place, or trying an adventurous activity for the first time.

Meeting a Role Model or Hero:

Experiencing excitement when meeting someone admired, like a favorite celebrity, an inspirational figure, or someone looked up to as a mentor or role model.

Excitement is a positive emotion often linked to anticipation, enthusiasm, and a sense of joy. It arises from positive events, achievements, or new experiences, making individuals feel energized, eager, and full of anticipation.

It brings about a heightened sense of anticipation, positive energy, and enthusiasm. This emotional state can:

Increase Positivity:

Excitement tends to boost overall positivity and optimism, shaping a more favorable mindset.

Enhance Motivation:

Feeling excited about a goal or activity can significantly increase motivation, making us more likely to pursue and achieve what we're excited about.

Improve Focus and Performance: Excitement can sharpen our focus and enhance performance by channeling our energy into the task at hand.

Elevate Mood:

The emotional high associated with excitement contributes to an elevated mood, creating a more joyful and upbeat mindset.

Strengthen Social Bonds:

Excitement is often contagious, and sharing exciting experiences with others can strengthen social bonds, fostering a positive and connected mindset.

In short, excitement brings a sense of joy and anticipation that positively influences our thoughts, feelings, and actions, creating a more motivated and optimistic mindset.

Jealousy/Envy:

These emotions can impact the mind negatively by causing comparison, insecurity, and a feeling of lack.

In Relationships:

Feeling jealous when a partner spends time with someone else or when someone shows interest in them, leading to feelings of insecurity or fear of losing the relationship.

Competitive Jealousy:

Feeling jealous of a colleague's success or recognition, especially when it seems to outshine one's own achievements, resulting in a desire to achieve a similar level of success.

Social Jealousy:

Feeling jealous of someone's popularity, social status, or the attention they receive, causing feelings of inadequacy or the desire to be similarly recognized.

Jealousy and envy are emotions that can have a negative impact on our mindset. Here's a simple explanation:

Comparison:

Jealousy and envy often arise when we compare ourselves to others, feeling that someone else has something we want or that we lack.

Negative Thoughts:

These emotions can lead to negative thoughts about ourselves and others. We might feel inferior, insecure, or resentful.

Impact on Self-Esteem:

Constantly feeling jealous or envious can harm our self-esteem, making us focus on what we lack rather than appreciating our own strengths and accomplishments.

Strained Relationships:

Jealousy can strain relationships, as it may lead to resentment and unhealthy competition with others.

Stagnation:

Instead of motivating positive change, jealousy can sometimes lead to a feeling of being stuck or powerless, thinking that we can't achieve what others have.

In simple terms, jealousy and envy create a mindset that is often centered on comparison, negativity, and dissatisfaction. It's important to manage these emotions, using them as signals to focus on personal growth rather than letting them negatively impact our thoughts and relationships.

We should remember that each emotion influences our thoughts, behavior, and overall mental state. Understanding and managing these emotions can play a vital role in maintaining good mental health. Recognizing and appropriately dealing with our emotions can contribute to a healthier and more balanced mindset.

CHAPTER 4
IMPACT OF WORRY & HOW TO MANAGE IT

"Worry" provides an opportunity to explore the nature of worrying, its impact on mindset, and strategies for managing or mitigating excessive worry. Here's a suggested structure for manging worry.

Worry" is a state of unease or anxiety, often accompanied by a sense of impending trouble or concern about potential future events. It involves dwelling on uncertainties, fears, or negative possibilities, and it can manifest as a series of repetitive and distressing thoughts. Worrying is a natural part of the human experience, but excessive or chronic worry can have detrimental effects on mental well-being and overall quality of life. It tends to focus on what might go wrong rather than on solutions or positive outcomes. Managing worry involves recognizing and addressing the underlying concerns, adopting coping strategies, and cultivating a mindset that promotes resilience and constructive problem-solving.

The Nature of Worry

Worry is like a little voice in your head that keeps telling you things might go wrong or that something bad might happen. It's like your mind playing out "what if" scenarios, and often, those scenarios are not positive.

Imagine you have a big test coming up. Instead of thinking, "I'll do my best and it will be okay," the worry might make you think, "What if I fail? What if I don't know the answers?" That's the nature of worry – it's the mind getting stuck on possible problems and uncertainties.

It's a bit like having a friend who always points out the negatives or the things that could go wrong, even if they haven't happened yet. Worry can make you feel uneasy, nervous, or stressed because it's focused on the idea that something bad might happen in the future.

The key is to recognize when worry is taking over and try to shift your thoughts to more positive and realistic ones.

It's like telling that worry voice, "Hey, I hear you, but let's also consider the good things that could happen."

The Impact on Mindset

Imagine your mind is like a garden. Your thoughts and feelings are the flowers and plants in that garden. Now, worry is like a weed – a pesky plant that can grow and take up space.

When you constantly worry, it's like letting those weeds take over your garden. They can crowd out the positive thoughts and make everything seem overwhelming. Your mindset, which is like the overall atmosphere of your mental garden, can become gloomy and stressed.

Worrying a lot can make you feel anxious, tense, and uneasy. It's like having a storm in your mental garden. The more you let worry grow, the stormier it gets.

On the other hand, if you try to manage your worries and focus on positive thoughts, it's like pulling out those weeds. Your mental garden becomes more pleasant, and your mindset becomes calmer and more positive.

So, the impact of worry on your mindset is like letting weeds take over your mental garden and create a storm, whereas managing worry is like tending to your garden and creating a more peaceful and positive atmosphere.

Understanding the Roots of Worry

Think of worry like a plant. The root cause of worry is like the seed you plant in the soil of your mind. This seed often comes from not knowing what's going to happen or being unsure about something.

So, the "soil" is uncertainty, and the "seed" is a thought that things might go wrong. When you keep thinking about this possibility, it's like watering the seed. The more attention you give to these thoughts, the more they grow into a big plant – let's call it the Worry Plant.

The Worry Plant has branches that are like all the "what-if" scenarios – imagining different ways things could go wrong. These branches can make you feel stressed or anxious, and that's the worry taking over.

To tackle worry, you need to be aware of the seed you're planting and try not to water it too much. Instead, focus on positive thoughts and possibilities. By doing this, you can prevent the worry plant from growing too big and keep your mental garden a bit more relaxed and happy.

Strategies for Managing Worry

Managing worry is like being a gardener in your mind. Here are some strategies, or gardening tips, to help you take care of your mental garden:

Imagine worry is like a weed in your mind. Pull out the negative thoughts, just like you would pull out weeds in a garden. Don't let them take up too much space.

Focus on positive thoughts. It's like giving water to the flowers in your mental garden. The more attention you give to good thoughts, the more they'll grow and push away the worries.

Sometimes worries get big because you're too close to them. Imagine stepping back and looking at the big picture, like getting some sunlight on your plants. It helps you see things more clearly.

Just like plants need care, your mind might need a bit of help too. Share your worries with someone you trust. It's like getting advice on how to take care of your mental garden.

Imagine planting seeds that can actually grow into strong plants. Set achievable goals and expectations for yourself. It's like planting seeds that you know will grow well.

Even the best gardeners need breaks. If your mind feels tired or overwhelmed, take a break. It's like letting your mental garden relax and breathe.

Remember, managing worry is about being a good gardener for your mind – pulling out the weeds, watering the good thoughts, and giving your mental garden the care it needs.

Embracing a Growth Mindset

Imagine your mindset as a way of thinking, like a set of beliefs in your brain.

Some people believe their abilities and intelligence are fixed – like they're set in stone. It's like thinking, "I'm only good at certain things, and that's it."

Others have a growth mindset. They believe they can improve and learn with effort and practice. It's like saying, "I might not be good at this now, but I can get better if I work at it."

Now, why is having a growth mindset important?

A growth mindset helps you see challenges as opportunities to learn and grow. Instead of thinking, "This is too hard," you say, "This is a chance for me to get better."

With a growth mindset, mistakes aren't the end of the world. They're stepping stones to improvement. It's like saying, "I didn't get it right this time, but I can figure it out next time."

Instead of thinking, "I either have it or I don't," a growth mindset says, "If I put in effort, I can get better." It's about believing in the power of hard work.

People with a growth mindset look at others' successes and think, "If they can do it, so can I." It's like being inspired by others and believing in your own potential.

So, having a growth mindset is like wearing a pair of glasses that helps you see challenges, mistakes, and effort in a positive light. It's a way of thinking that says, "I can improve, learn, and grow over time."

Let us conduct a case study for Embracing a Growth Mindset in Jaihar Village:

Jaihar, an Indian village, faced a common challenge seen in many communities – individuals with fixed mindsets believing their abilities were limited. Aanya, a young girl with a passion for art, reflected this mindset, feeling inadequate compared to her peers.

Jaihar hosted an annual art competition, but Aanya hesitated to participate due to her fixed mindset. The village teacher, Mr. Sharma, noticed this trend among the students and saw an opportunity to introduce the concept of a growth mindset.

Mr. Sharma shared a story of a renowned artist who, despite starting with basic skills, became a master through dedication and practice. He introduced the idea that abilities can be developed through embracing challenges, learning from mistakes, and putting in effort.

Inspired by this new perspective, Aanya decided to change her mindset. She embraced the challenge of the art competition as an opportunity to learn and grow. She practiced diligently, sought guidance from Mr. Sharma, and learned from her peers.

Aanya's transformation became a village sensation. While she didn't win the competition, the judges praised her effort and improvement. This success story inspired other children in Jaihar to adopt a growth mindset. The village school witnessed a positive shift in attitude and approach to challenges.

Over the years, Aanya continued honing her artistic skills and became a mentor to younger children. The village of Jaihar became renowned not only for its annual art competition but for fostering a culture of growth mindset. The community now believes that with effort and dedication, continuous learning and improvement are achievable.

Conclusion:

Jaihar's case demonstrates the transformative power of embracing a growth mindset. Through a simple shift in perspective, the village not only saw individual improvements but also cultivated a culture of continuous learning and development. The journey of Aanya and her peers serves as a compelling example for other communities seeking to foster a growth mindset.

Let us embrace the powerful message of hope and empowerment. The journey of managing worry and transforming mindset is indeed challenging, but it carries the promise of growth and resilience. Just as a diligent gardener tends to their garden, we too can nurture our minds, pulling out the weeds of worry and watering the flowers of positivity.

Remember, worry is not a permanent resident in our minds. It's a passing cloud that can be replaced with the sunlight of hope and empowerment. By adopting strategies to manage worry, we take charge of our mental garden, allowing the seeds of positive thoughts to blossom.

As we navigate the twists and turns of life, let us hold onto the belief that worry can be managed, and our mindset can be transformed. The power to cultivate hope and empower ourselves lies within, ready to guide us towards a brighter and more resilient future.

CHAPTER 5
EGO AND ATTITUDE

EGO

In simple terms, the ego is like the image you have of yourself—the way you see and value who you are. It's like your personal identity or how you view your own importance. If someone says another person has a "big ego," it means they think highly of themselves, sometimes to the point of being a bit too proud or self-centered. So, in everyday language, ego is about how you see yourself and how much you think of yourself.

It's important to note that the term "ego" can have slightly different nuances depending on the field of study or cultural context in which it is used.

Ego refers to a person's sense of self-importance or self-esteem. The impact of ego on mindset is how it can shape the way someone thinks and behaves.

Positive Impact:

A healthy ego can give a person confidence and a positive self-image. It can drive individuals to set and achieve goals, take on challenges, and believe in their abilities.

Imagine your mind is like a superhero that helps you feel good about yourself. This superhero is your positive ego.

Here's how it works:

Confidence Booster: Positive ego is like your personal cheerleader. It gives you the confidence to take on challenges and believe in your abilities. It's like having a friend in your head saying, "You can do it!"

Goal Achiever: Positive ego helps you set goals and work towards them. It's the voice in your mind saying, "I can make this happen." This superhero mindset encourages you to reach for the stars.

Mood Lifter: When you're feeling down, your positive ego comes to the rescue. It reminds you of your strengths and achievements, making you feel better about yourself. It's like a mood-boosting sidekick.

Friend Magnet: People like being around someone with a positive ego. It's like a magnetic force that attracts friends because you radiate good vibes and make others feel good too.

So, in simple words, having a positive ego is like having a friendly superhero in your mind that cheers you on, helps you achieve your dreams, lifts your spirits when you're down, and makes you someone others want to be around. It's the key to feeling good about yourself and the world around you.

Negative Impact: On the flip side, if someone has an overly inflated ego, it can lead to arrogance or a sense of superiority. This might make it difficult for them to accept feedback or acknowledge their mistakes because they want to maintain a perfect image.

Imagine negative ego as a grumpy villain in your mind. Here's how it causes trouble:

Overconfidence: Negative ego makes you think you're better than everyone else. It's like a bossy voice saying, "I'm always right," which can lead to problems because you might not listen to others.

Fear of Mistakes: This villain hates admitting when you're wrong. So, instead of learning from mistakes, negative ego makes you avoid them or blame others. It's like a stubborn sidekick that refuses to see any flaws.

Isolation: Negative ego can push people away. It's like a friend-repelling force because if you act like you're always superior, it's hard for others to connect with you.

Difficulty in Learning: The villain of negative ego doesn't like learning from others. It thinks it knows everything already, making it tough to grow and improve. It's like a closed door to new ideas.

In short, negative ego is like a grumpy character causing problems by making you too bossy, afraid of mistakes, pushing people away, and resisting learning from others. It's the opposite of the friendly superhero we want in our minds.

Impact on Relationships: Ego can affect how people interact with others. If someone's ego is too strong, they might struggle with empathy, compromise, or understanding different perspectives. This can lead to conflicts in relationships.

Confidence and Self-Respect: A healthy ego can contribute to your self-esteem, making you more confident in your interactions with friends, family, and relatives.

Assertiveness: It helps you express your thoughts and needs clearly without being overly submissive or dominant, fostering open communication.

Mutual Respect: A balanced ego allows you to appreciate the strengths and accomplishments of others, promoting mutual respect within relationships.

Supportive Relationships: Having a positive sense of self-worth can lead to more supportive and fulfilling relationships, as you are better able to contribute positively to the well-being of those around you.

Negative Impact of Ego:

Conflict and Tension: An inflated or negative ego can lead to conflicts and tension within relationships, as it may cause you to be overly competitive, dismissive, or critical.

Difficulty in Apologizing: Negative ego traits, such as stubbornness or a fear of being perceived as wrong, can make it challenging to apologize, potentially straining relationships.

Lack of Empathy: If ego dominates, it may hinder your ability to empathize with the feelings and perspectives of friends, family, and relatives, leading to misunderstandings.

Isolation: Excessive ego can make it difficult to collaborate and compromise, potentially isolating you from those you care about.

Openness to Learning: A person with a balanced ego is generally more open to learning and adapting. They can accept that they don't know everything and are willing to learn from others. On the other hand, a person with a big ego might be resistant to new ideas or suggestions that challenge their sense of superiority.

Our ego plays a significant role in shaping our mindset. A healthy balance is essential for personal growth, positive relationships, and a willingness to learn from various experiences.

The impact of ego on relationships with friends, family, and relatives mirrors its impact on relationships in general. A healthy ego fosters positive interactions, while a negative or inflated ego can lead to conflicts, difficulties in apologizing, a lack of empathy, and potential isolation within these important connections

Let us explore Positive and Nagative Ego though following Examples :-

Scenario: Team Success at Work

Imagine you're part of a project team at your workplace, and the team has successfully completed a challenging project. Here's how positive ego might manifest:

Positive Ego Response: Colleague: "Wow, the project was a huge success! Great job, everyone!"

You (with positive ego): "Thank you! I appreciate the recognition. It was truly a team effort. Each team member played a crucial role, and I'm grateful to have such a talented and dedicated group working together. Let's celebrate our success together!"

In this example, the person acknowledges the praise with gratitude, emphasizes the collaborative effort, and highlights the contributions of the entire team. This response demonstrates confidence, appreciation for others, and a positive mindset that values teamwork and shared success.

Scenario: Team Success at Work

Colleague: "Wow, the project was a huge success! Great job, everyone!"

Person (with negative ego): "Well, obviously. I was the driving force behind it. Without my expertise and hard work, this project wouldn't have gone anywhere. I pretty much carried the team."

In this example, the person responds with a negative ego by dismissing the contributions of others, taking sole credit for the success, and downplaying the role of the team. This response is characterized by arrogance, a lack of humility, and an inflated sense of self-importance. It can create tension within the team and negatively impact collaboration and morale.

ATTITUDE

Our attitude is the product of both positive and negative emotions and energies. Being positive means having a positive attitude. An attitude is a forceful tool in our hands that can cause both success and failure. All around us, we hear judgments about others floating around – he has an inflated ego, she has a quick temper, he is sincere, she is hard working, he is a man of principles, she is honest, and so on. We usually do not stop and think about why a person is tagged in a certain way. Reputation develops over time. When you demonstrate a particular attitude for some time, it slowly becomes your identity. Just like everyone else, we too would have some labels attached to us. Our attitude defines our image in society. People dealing with us tend to work with us as per our image. If our image is that of an honest person, they would put more faith in us. On the contrary, if our image is negative, they will always be on their guards. Therefore, it is important to build and protect your image with care.

Attitude refers to a person's overall outlook, feelings, and mindset toward something or someone. It involves a combination of beliefs, emotions, and behaviors that shape how an individual perceives and responds to situations, people, or events. Attitude can be positive, negative, or neutral, and it plays a significant role in influencing one's thoughts, actions, and interactions with the world.

Factors that impact our Attitude

Several factors contribute to the formation of our attitudes. These factors can be shaped by personal experiences, social influences, and individual characteristics. Here are some key factors:

Personal Experiences: Our past experiences significantly influence our attitudes. Positive or negative encounters with people, events, or situations can shape how we perceive similar situations in the future.

Example: Overcoming a Professional Setback

Imagine you're working on a significant project at your job, and despite your best efforts, it doesn't go as planned. The project may face unexpected challenges, timelines might not be met, and the end result may not be as successful as you had hoped.

Fixed Mindset Reaction: If you have a fixed mindset, you might interpret the setback as a reflection of your abilities. Thoughts like, "I'm not cut out for this," or "I've failed, and there's no recovering from this" may dominate your thinking. This mindset could lead to feelings of defeat and reluctance to take on similar challenges in the future.

Growth Mindset Reaction: On the other hand, if you have a growth mindset, you may view the setback as a temporary obstacle and an opportunity for learning. You might think, "This project didn't go as planned, but I can learn from what went wrong," or "I'll use this experience to improve my skills and approach next time." With a growth mindset, setbacks are seen as a natural part of the learning and development process.

The way you interpret and respond to professional setbacks can significantly influence your future endeavours. A growth mindset fosters resilience, adaptability, and a willingness to learn from failures, ultimately contributing to personal and professional development.

In this example, the personal experience of facing a professional setback illustrates how one's mindset can shape their response to challenges and impact their ability to bounce back, learn, and grow in their career.

Cultural Background: The culture we grow up in and the values it holds play a crucial role in shaping our attitudes. Cultural norms and beliefs influence our views on various aspects of life.

Example: Communication Styles

Imagine you grew up in a culture where indirect communication is the norm. In such a culture, individuals may use subtle cues, non-verbal expressions, or implied messages to convey their thoughts and feelings. Openly expressing disagreement or giving direct feedback might be considered impolite or confrontational.

Now, suppose you find yourself in a work or social environment that values and encourages direct communication. People express their opinions openly, provide constructive criticism directly, and expect others to do the same.

Cultural Influence on Mindset: If your cultural background encourages indirect communication, you might initially find the direct and explicit communication style uncomfortable or even confrontational. You may interpret straightforward feedback as rude or insensitive. This could influence your mindset, making you hesitant to express your opinions openly or to provide direct feedback, even when it's expected in the new environment.

Adaptation and Mindset Shift: Over time, as you navigate this new cultural context, you may gradually adapt your communication style. Initially, it might be challenging, but with exposure and understanding, you might come to appreciate the benefits of direct communication. Your mindset evolves, and you become more open to expressing your thoughts directly and receiving feedback without perceiving it as a personal attack.

In this example, the impact of cultural background on mindset is evident in how communication styles are perceived and navigated. Awareness of these cultural influences can lead to a more flexible mindset, allowing individuals to adapt to different cultural contexts and communication norms. This adaptation highlights the dynamic nature of mindset and its responsiveness to cultural experiences.

Social Influences: The people around us, such as family, friends, peers, and society, have a profound impact on our attitudes. We often adopt the attitudes of those we are close to or respect.

Example: Career Choices and Social Expectations

Imagine you are a young individual deciding on your career path. Your family and society place a high value on traditional, prestigious professions like medicine, law, or engineering. There is a prevailing belief that success is primarily defined by pursuing these established careers.

Social Influence on Mindset: The societal expectations and the influence of your family can shape your mindset, leading you to believe that choosing a career outside these conventional paths might be met with disapproval or skepticism. The prevailing attitude emphasizes stability, financial success, and societal recognition associated with these professions.

Initial Career Choice: Under the influence of these expectations, you may initially lean towards a career in medicine, even if your true interests and passions lie in a different field. The fear of societal judgment and the desire for approval from family and peers may strongly influence your decision-making process.

Impact on Well-being: As you pursue a career in medicine to meet societal expectations, you may find yourself feeling unfulfilled and stressed. The misalignment between your true interests and the chosen path can have a negative impact on your mental well-being and job satisfaction.

Mindset Shift: Over time, with exposure to diverse perspectives and experiences, you may encounter individuals who have found success and fulfillment in non-traditional careers. This exposure challenges the societal norms ingrained in your mindset. As you gain a broader understanding of success and happiness, your mindset shifts, allowing you to reconsider your career choices based on your true interests and passion rather than solely on societal expectations.

In this example, social influence, including family expectations and societal norms, initially guides your career choices and shapes your mindset. However, as you gain exposure to different perspectives and experiences, your mindset becomes more flexible, allowing you to reassess your values and make choices that align with your personal fulfillment and well-being. This illustrates how social influence can significantly impact our mindset, shaping our beliefs and decisions in various aspects of life.

Education and Upbringing: The values instilled in us through education and upbringing contribute to our attitudes. Moral and ethical teachings from parents, teachers, and mentors can shape our perspective on right and wrong.

Media and Mass Communication: Exposure to media, including television, movies, books, and social media, can shape our attitudes by influencing our perceptions of the world and shaping our beliefs about certain issues.

Personality Traits: Individual personality characteristics, such as openness, conscientiousness, and agreeableness, can influence the formation of attitudes. For example, a more open-minded person might have a more flexible attitude.

Example: Dealing with Setbacks

Imagine you have a personality trait that leans towards resilience and optimism. You generally see setbacks as temporary and surmountable challenges rather than insurmountable obstacles.

Resilient Personality Trait: Your natural inclination is to view difficulties as opportunities for growth. When faced with a setback, such as not getting a desired promotion at work, your mindset is framed by resilience. You might think, "This setback is tough, but it's a chance to learn and improve. I'll work harder and seize the next opportunity."

Impact on Mindset: Your resilient personality trait influences your mindset in a positive way. Instead of dwelling on failure or feeling defeated, you are more likely to approach challenges with a growth mindset. You see setbacks as part of the journey and believe in your ability to overcome obstacles through effort and learning.

Adaptability: This mindset allows you to adapt more easily to changes and uncertainties. You may seek feedback, identify areas for improvement, and adjust your approach accordingly. Your optimistic outlook helps you maintain a positive attitude, fostering a mindset that sees setbacks as stepping stones rather than roadblocks.

Now, let's consider a contrasting personality trait

Pessimistic Personality Trait: On the other hand, if you have a more pessimistic personality trait, setbacks may deeply impact your mindset. You might be more prone to negative thoughts, such as "I always fail," or "I'll never succeed in my career." This mindset can lead to a cycle of self-doubt and reluctance to take on new challenges.

Impact on Mindset: The pessimistic mindset may hinder your ability to bounce back from setbacks. Instead of seeing challenges as opportunities, you might view them as confirmation of your perceived limitations. This fixed mindset can affect your confidence, motivation, and willingness to take risks.

In this example, the impact of personality traits on mindset is evident in how individuals with different traits approach and navigate setbacks. A resilient and optimistic personality fosters a growth mindset, enabling individuals to see challenges as opportunities for improvement. Conversely, a more pessimistic personality may contribute to a fixed mindset, where setbacks are seen as permanent and discouraging. Understanding and being aware of our personality traits can provide insights into how we perceive and respond to various situations in life.

Let's consider a scenario in which someone with a pessimistic mindset approaches a new job opportunity.

Imagine there's a person named Alex who recently received a job interview invitation for a position he has been interested in. A pessimistic mindset might lead Alex to immediately focus on the negative aspects of the situation. Here's how their thought process might unfold:

Negative Anticipation: Alex might start by thinking, "I'll probably mess up the interview. I never do well in these situations."

Catastrophizing: Instead of viewing the interview as a chance to showcase his skills, the pessimistic mindset leads Alex to imagine the worst-case scenario. He might think, "If I don't get this job, my career is over. I'll never find another opportunity like this."

Discounting Positive Aspects: Even if Alex has relevant qualifications and experiences, a pessimistic mindset may cause them to downplay their achievements. They might say, "Sure, I have some experience, but there are probably other candidates who are way more qualified."

Self-Fulfilling Prophecy: With a negative mindset, Alex might convey low confidence during the interview, affecting his performance. This, in turn, could lead to the outcome he feared – not getting the job.

Rumination: After the interview, a pessimistic person might dwell on every perceived mistake, thinking, "I knew I shouldn't have said that. It's no wonder they won't hire me."

This example illustrates how a pessimistic mindset can shape thoughts and behaviors in a way that reinforces negativity and increases the likelihood of negative outcomes. It's important to note that mindset can significantly influence one's experiences and reactions to various situations.

Self-Reflection and Awareness: Personal reflection and self-awareness play a role in shaping attitudes. Being conscious of one's thoughts, values, and beliefs allows for intentional attitude development.

Imagine you often find yourself in conflicts with friends or family members due to communication issues. Without self-reflection and awareness, your mindset might be fixed on blaming others or external circumstances for these conflicts.

Lack of Self-Reflection: Initially, you might approach conflicts with thoughts like, "They never understand me," or "I'm always the one who has to compromise." This mindset can lead to a pattern of recurring conflicts, as it doesn't allow for personal growth or an understanding of your role in the dynamics.

Impact on Relationships: The lack of self-reflection and awareness can strain relationships. Your fixed mindset may prevent you from seeing opportunities for personal development and hinder your ability to empathize with others' perspectives.

Now, let's consider the impact of self-reflection and awareness on mindset.

Introduction of Self-Reflection: Recognizing the recurring conflicts, you decide to engage in self-reflection. You ask yourself questions like, "How do I contribute to these conflicts?" and "What patterns do I notice in my communication style?"

Awareness and Mindset Shift: Through self-reflection, you become more aware of your communication patterns, emotional triggers, and the impact of your words on others. This newfound awareness leads to a mindset shift where you take responsibility for your role in conflicts and recognize the potential for personal growth.

Positive Impact: Equipped with this awareness, you start implementing changes in your communication style. You become more open to understanding others' perspectives, expressing yourself more clearly, and actively listening. The mindset shift from blaming external factors to taking responsibility for your actions fosters healthier relationships and contributes to personal development.

In this example, self-reflection and awareness play a crucial role in shifting the mindset from a fixed, blame-oriented perspective to a more growth-oriented one. By understanding and addressing one's own contributions to conflicts, individuals can foster personal growth and improve the quality of their interpersonal relationships.

Peer Pressure: The influence of peers and the desire to fit in can impact our attitudes. Sometimes, individuals adopt certain attitudes to align with the opinions of their peer group.

Example: Decision-Making and Peer Pressure

Imagine you're a high school student faced with the decision of whether to participate in an after-school activity that aligns with your personal interests or to join a group of peers who are pressuring you to engage in activities that don't resonate with your values.

Peer Pressure on Attitude: Your friends are enthusiastic about a particular extracurricular activity that may involve behaviors or actions that make you uncomfortable. The pressure from your peers can affect your attitude, making you question whether sticking to your own interests is worth potential social exclusion or disapproval.

Initial Attitude: Before the influence of peer pressure, you may have had a positive attitude toward pursuing your own interests and passions. You valued individuality and were excited about the prospect of joining a club related to your personal hobbies or skills.

Impact of Peer Pressure: As the pressure from your peers increases, you may start to experience a shift in attitude. The fear of not fitting in or being judged may make you more receptive to their suggestions, leading to a negative impact on your initial positive attitude.

Decision-Making and Attitude Shift: In this scenario, if you succumb to peer pressure, your attitude toward the after-school activity may become more negative. You might feel conflicted, knowing that you are compromising your true interests and values to conform to your peers' expectations.

Potential Consequences: Depending on the degree of influence, the negative attitude resulting from peer pressure may not only impact your immediate decision but could also affect your overall well-being. You might feel a sense of dissonance between your true self and the choices you're making to fit in with your peers.

It's important to note that while peer pressure can influence attitudes and decisions, individuals may also develop strategies to resist such pressure and maintain authenticity in their attitudes and choices. This example illustrates how external influences, in this case, peer pressure, can impact our attitudes and decision-making processes, emphasizing the need for self-awareness and assertiveness in maintaining individual values and perspectives.

Economic Factors: Socioeconomic status and financial stability can influence attitudes. For instance, economic hardships or prosperity may shape one's views on issues related to wealth and poverty.

Let's consider real-life examples to illustrate how economic factors impact attitudes and mindsets:

During Economic Boom:

Example: In the mid-2000s, before the global financial crisis, many people experienced a period of economic prosperity. Home values were rising, job opportunities were abundant, and the stock market was doing well.

Impact on Attitude: During this time, individuals were optimistic about the future. Many were confident in the stability of their jobs, leading to positive attitudes towards spending and investment. Homeownership rates increased as people believed in the value of real estate as an investment.

After the 2008 Financial Crisis:

Example: Following the 2008 financial crisis, the global economy faced a severe downturn. Many people lost their jobs, and there was a significant decline in housing values and stock prices.

Impact on Attitude: The economic downturn led to widespread insecurity. Individuals became more cautious about their spending, prioritized saving, and were hesitant to take on financial risks. Attitudes shifted towards job security, with many focusing on maintaining their current employment rather than pursuing career advancements.

COVID-19 Pandemic:

Example: The COVID-19 pandemic, starting in 2019, caused widespread economic disruptions globally. Lockdowns and restrictions led to job losses, business closures, and an overall economic downturn.

Impact on Attitude: The pandemic resulted in heightened economic insecurity. Many individuals faced job losses or income reductions, leading to a more pessimistic outlook. People became cautious about spending, focusing on essential needs, and adopting a conservative approach to their finances.

Post-Recession Recovery:

Example: After a period of economic recession, governments often implement measures to stimulate recovery, such as lowering interest rates and increasing spending on infrastructure projects.

Impact on Attitude: As the economy starts to recover, individuals may experience a gradual improvement in their attitudes. The return of job opportunities and economic stability can lead to increased optimism, with people regaining confidence in their financial future. This may result in a shift towards more positive spending and investment behaviors.

These real-life examples demonstrate how economic factors, whether positive or negative, have tangible effects on people's attitudes and mindsets. Economic conditions influence perceptions of job security, optimism about the future, and financial behaviors in practical and measurable ways.

Age and Life Stage: Attitudes can change over the course of a person's life. Different life stages, such as adolescence, adulthood, and old age, can bring about shifts in attitudes due to changing priorities and experiences.

Let's explore a real-life example of how age and life stage can impact attitudes and mindsets:

Example: Millennials and Homeownership

Age and Life Stage Context:

Millennials are a generation born roughly between 1981 and 1996. As of the early 2020s, many Millennials have entered adulthood, establishing careers, and starting families.

Attitude and Mindset Impact:

Attitude in Early Adulthood (20s and early 30s):

Attitude: During their early adult years, many Millennials faced economic challenges such as student loan debt, high housing costs, and a competitive job market.

Impact: The economic realities led to a delayed entry into homeownership compared to previous generations. Millennials, during this life stage, often had attitudes characterized by a preference for flexibility, experiences over possessions, and a focus on career development.

Attitude in Mid to Late Adulthood (late 30s and 40s):

Attitude: As Millennials progressed into their late 30s and 40s, many experienced career advancements, increased income, and a shift in priorities, often including a desire for stability and family-oriented goals.

Impact: The attitude towards homeownership shifted for some. Many started viewing homeownership as a means of providing stability for their families and building equity. There was a shift from the earlier preference for renting and mobility to a desire for a more permanent and secure living situation.

Factors Influencing the Shift:

Economic Stability: As Millennials advanced in their careers and experienced increased economic stability, the attitude towards long-term investments, such as homeownership, became more positive.

Life Stage Changes: Life events such as getting married, starting a family, or desiring more space for a growing family influenced the mindset towards homeownership. The need for stability and a sense of permanence became more pronounced.

Conclusion: The example illustrates how age and life stage impact attitudes and mindsets. In early adulthood, economic challenges and different priorities can shape a preference for flexibility and experiences. However, as individuals progress through life stages, economic stability and changing priorities can lead to shifts in attitudes, such as a greater emphasis on stability and a positive view of long-term investments like homeownership. This real-life example highlights the dynamic nature of attitudes influenced by age and life stage.

Understanding that attitudes are influenced by a combination of these factors can help individuals become more aware of their own perspectives and be open to considering different viewpoints.

Imagine Your Mind as a Garden:

Attitude as the Soil: Your attitude is like the soil in your mental garden. If it's good, your mindset plants positive thoughts. If it's not so good, negative thoughts might take root.

Positive Attitude as Fertile Soil: A positive attitude is like fertile soil. It helps your mindset grow flowers of optimism, resilience, and happiness. You see challenges as opportunities and setbacks as temporary.

Negative Attitude as Poor Soil: On the other hand, a negative attitude is like poor soil. It can make your mindset grow weeds of doubt, stress, and negativity. Challenges seem overwhelming, and it's harder to see the bright side.

Impact on Growth: Just as good soil helps plants thrive, a positive attitude helps your mindset flourish. It nurtures a mindset that's open to learning, resilient in the face of difficulties, and appreciative of the good things.

In Simple Words:

Positive Attitude: It's like having rich, nurturing soil. Your mindset garden is full of vibrant, colorful flowers that make you feel good and ready to face the day.

Negative Attitude: It's like having poor, dry soil. Weeds of negativity can take over, making your mindset feel heavy and making it harder to find joy in everyday things.

So, your attitude is like the soil that influences what grows in your mental garden. A positive attitude helps your mindset thrive, while a negative attitude can hinder its growth.

CHAPTER 6
STRUGGLES IN LIFE

The impact of life struggles on our mindset is profound and can shape the way we perceive the world, handle challenges, and approach various aspects of life. Here's how life struggles can influence our mindset:

Resilience and Strength:

Impact: Going through life struggles often builds resilience. It's like developing a kind of mental toughness that helps us bounce back from difficulties.

Example: Imagine facing a tough situation at work or in personal relationships. Overcoming these struggles can make you more resilient, better equipped to handle future challenges.

Let's consider an example that illustrates resilience and strength in the face of life struggles:

Example: Overcoming Job Loss

Life Struggle: Job Loss Imagine someone who unexpectedly loses their job due to company downsizing. This is a significant life struggle that can bring about financial stress, uncertainty about the future, and potential emotional strain.

Resilience and Strength in Action:

Facing the Reality: Resilience: Instead of letting the job loss overwhelm them, the person acknowledges the reality of the situation. Resilience is evident in their ability to confront the challenge rather than avoid it.

Adapting to Change:

Strength: The individual displays strength by quickly adapting to the new circumstances. They update their resume, actively seek new job opportunities, and explore potential career changes. This strength is reflected in their proactive response to the unexpected change.

Seeking Support: Resilience: Rather than isolating themselves, the person reaches out for support. Resilience is evident in their ability to recognize the importance of emotional and practical assistance during challenging times.

Learning and Growth:

Strength: The individual views the job loss not just as a setback but as an opportunity for growth. They might take this time to enhance their skills, explore new career paths, or pursue further education. Strength is demonstrated in their commitment to personal and professional development.

Maintaining a Positive Outlook:

Resilience: Despite the difficulties, the person maintains a positive outlook. Resilience is evident in their ability to find silver linings, such as increased time for family, personal projects, or pursuing passions.

Outcome: The individual, through a combination of resilience and strength, secures a new job that aligns better with their long-term goals. The experience of overcoming job loss has not only led to professional growth but has also strengthened their ability to handle future challenges.

Summary: This example illustrates resilience through facing the reality of the situation, seeking support, and maintaining a positive outlook. Strength is demonstrated in adapting to change, actively pursuing opportunities for growth, and turning the challenge into a stepping stone for personal and professional development. Together, resilience and strength enable the individual to navigate the life struggle of job loss and emerge stronger on the other side.

Perspective on Challenges:

Impact: Life struggles can change how we see challenges. It's like shifting from seeing them as roadblocks to viewing them as opportunities for growth.

Example: After facing a difficult period, you might start seeing challenges as a chance to learn and improve, rather than as purely negative experiences.

Let's explore an example that demonstrates how one's perspective on challenges can evolve during life struggles:

Example: Coping with a Chronic Illness

Life Struggle: Chronic Illness Diagnosis Imagine someone receiving a diagnosis of a chronic illness that requires long-term management and lifestyle adjustments. This situation presents a significant life struggle, as it involves adapting to changes in health, potential limitations, and ongoing medical care.

Evolution of Perspective on Challenges:

Initial Reaction: Early Perspective: Initially, the person may feel overwhelmed and view the chronic illness as an insurmountable challenge. The focus might be on the limitations and disruptions it brings to daily life.

Educating Oneself:

Shift in Perspective: Over time, the individual starts educating themselves about the illness, treatment options, and ways to manage symptoms. The perspective begins to shift from seeing only the negative aspects to understanding the condition and potential strategies for improvement.

Mindset Transformation:

Shift in Perspective: As the person learns more about their condition, they begin to view it not just as a challenge but as an opportunity for personal growth and resilience. The perspective evolves from a purely negative view to one that recognizes the potential for learning and adaptation.

Community Engagement:

Shift in Perspective: Engaging with others who share similar health challenges introduces a new perspective. The individual starts seeing the shared experiences within a community, fostering a sense of support and understanding. The focus shifts from isolation to a shared journey.

Embracing a New Normal:

Shift in Perspective: The person starts adapting to the new normal, incorporating lifestyle changes, and finding joy in small victories. The perspective on the challenge transforms from seeing it as a constant burden to recognizing the resilience and strength developed through adaptation.

Outcome: While the chronic illness remains a part of the person's life, the evolved perspective allows them to lead a fulfilling life despite the challenges. The individual has not only learned to manage the health condition but has also developed a positive outlook on life, emphasizing growth and the ability to overcome adversity.

Summary: This example illustrates the evolution of perspective on challenges during a life struggle. Initially, the focus may be on the difficulties, but over time, education, mindset transformation, community engagement, and adaptation contribute to a more positive and growth-oriented view of the situation.

Adaptability and Flexibility:

Impact: Life struggles can enhance our adaptability. It's like becoming more flexible in dealing with unexpected changes and uncertainties.

Example: Going through financial difficulties might teach you to adapt your spending habits, becoming more flexible with your budget when needed.

Let's explore an example that illustrates adaptability and flexibility in the face of life

Struggles:

Example: Navigating Unemployment and Career Change

Life Struggle: Job Loss and Career Uncertainty

Imagine someone unexpectedly losing their job due to company restructuring. This situation introduces a significant life struggle, involving financial uncertainty, potential changes in lifestyle, and the need to navigate a new career path.

Demonstrating Adaptability and Flexibility:

Assessing Skills and Interests:

Adaptability: Instead of fixating on the loss, the individual takes a proactive approach. They assess their skills, interests, and strengths. This adaptability allows them to identify transferable skills and explore new career possibilities.

Exploring Diverse Opportunities:

Flexibility: Rather than limiting themselves to a specific industry or role, the person remains open to diverse opportunities. Their flexibility allows them to consider different sectors, roles, or even entrepreneurship as potential paths forward.

Acquiring New Skills:

Adaptability: Recognizing the evolving job market, the individual invests time in acquiring new skills or enhancing existing ones. This adaptability not only broadens their skill set but also demonstrates a willingness to grow and adapt to changing circumstances.

Networking and Seeking Support:

Flexibility: Understanding the importance of networking, the individual actively reaches out to contacts in various fields. This flexibility in seeking support and connections increases the chances of discovering new career possibilities outside their initial comfort zone.

Considering Remote Work:

Adaptability: With the rise of remote work opportunities, the person considers job opportunities beyond their immediate geographic location. This adaptability to the changing nature of work allows them to explore a wider range of potential roles. In other words it is a type "Work from Home opportunity)

Outcome: Through a combination of adaptability and flexibility, the individual not only secures a new job but discovers a career path that aligns better with their skills and passions. The life struggle of job loss transforms into an opportunity for career growth and personal development.

Summary: This example demonstrates how adaptability and flexibility play crucial roles in navigating life struggles. By assessing skills, remaining open to diverse opportunities, acquiring new skills, seeking support, and adapting to changes in the job market, the individual turns a challenging situation into a catalyst for positive career transformation.

Gratitude and Appreciation:

Impact: Struggles can make us appreciate the good times more. It's like developing a sense of gratitude for the positive aspects of life.

Example: If you've experienced health challenges, you may have a heightened appreciation for good health during times of wellness.

Let's explore an example that illustrates gratitude and appreciation in the context of life struggles:

Example: Finding Gratitude After Financial Setbacks

Life Struggle: Financial Setbacks and Job Loss Imagine someone experiencing a period of financial struggles, including job loss and unexpected expenses. This situation introduces significant challenges, such as managing bills, providing for the family, and navigating uncertainties.

Cultivating Gratitude and Appreciation:

Acknowledging Support Systems:

Gratitude: Instead of solely focusing on the financial difficulties, the individual takes time to acknowledge the support systems around them. This gratitude extends to family, friends, and community resources that provide emotional support and assistance during tough times.

Finding Joy in Small Victories:

Appreciation: Despite the financial constraints, the person learns to find joy in small victories. This appreciation for simple pleasures, like spending quality time with family or enjoying low-cost activities, becomes a source of resilience and positivity.

Recognizing Learning Opportunities:

Gratitude: Rather than dwelling on setbacks, the individual expresses gratitude for the learning opportunities embedded in the challenges. The experience becomes a chance to develop financial literacy, budgeting skills, and a deeper understanding of personal priorities.

Volunteering and Giving Back:

Appreciation: To channel their gratitude into positive action, the person engages in volunteer work or community service. This appreciation for the support received motivates them to give back and contribute to the well-being of others facing similar struggles.

Focusing on Health and Relationships:

Gratitude: Amidst financial challenges, the individual expresses gratitude for the health of themselves and their loved ones. This perspective shift highlights the importance of non-material aspects of life and fosters a deeper appreciation for relationships and well-being.

Outcome: Through the cultivation of gratitude and appreciation, the person not only navigates the financial struggles with resilience but also emerges from the experience with a heightened sense of gratitude for the supportive relationships, the lessons learned, and the non-material aspects of life.

Summary: This example illustrates how gratitude and appreciation can be cultivated during life struggles. By acknowledging support systems, finding joy in small victories, recognizing learning opportunities, engaging in acts of kindness, and appreciating non-material aspects of life, individuals can shift their mindset and find positivity even in challenging circumstances.

Empathy and Understanding:

Impact: Life struggles often foster empathy. It's like gaining a better understanding of others who may be going through difficult times.

Example: Having faced personal loss might make you more empathetic towards others experiencing grief.

Let's explore an example that demonstrates empathy and understanding in the context of life struggles:

Example: Building Empathy Through Personal Loss

Life Struggle: Coping with Personal Loss

Imagine someone going through the profound and challenging experience of losing a loved one. This situation represents a significant life struggle, involving grief, emotional pain, and the need to navigate life without the presence of someone dear.

Expressing Empathy and Understanding:

Connecting with Others in Grief: Empathy: Instead of isolating themselves in grief, the person seeks connections with others who have experienced similar losses. This empathy allows them to share experiences, offer and receive support, and understand the universality of grief.

Listening and Validation:

Understanding: Friends and family provide a supportive environment where the person feels heard and understood. Through active listening and validation, loved ones demonstrate an understanding of the individual's emotions and struggles.

Acknowledging Different Grieving Processes:

Empathy: Recognizing that everyone grieves differently, the person develops empathy for others who may be processing grief in unique ways. This understanding helps foster compassion and tolerance for diverse grieving processes.

Supporting Others in Times of Need:

Empathy: The individual, drawing from their own experiences, becomes a source of empathy for others going through similar losses. Their understanding of the pain and challenges enables them to offer genuine support and comfort.

Advocating for Mental Health Awareness:

Understanding: In the process of healing, the person becomes an advocate for mental health awareness, recognizing the importance of understanding and addressing the emotional toll of grief. Their empathy extends to creating awareness and fostering understanding in the broader community.

Outcome: Through the expression of empathy and understanding, the individual not only navigates their own grief but becomes a source of support for others facing similar struggles. The shared experiences contribute to a sense of community and mutual understanding surrounding the complexities of loss.

Summary: This example highlights how empathy and understanding can be cultivated through life struggles, particularly in the context of personal loss. By connecting with others in similar situations, listening with empathy, acknowledging diverse grieving processes, supporting others, and advocating for mental health awareness, individuals can foster a deeper understanding of the shared human experience of grief.

Goal Setting and Motivation:

Impact: Overcoming struggles can fuel goal-setting and motivation. It's like using past challenges as motivation to achieve new objectives.

Example: After overcoming a career setback, you may set new career goals and work towards them with renewed determination.

Let's explore an example of goal setting and motivation in a context other than health issues:

Example: Overcoming Financial Setbacks

Life Struggle: Dealing with Financial Hardship

Imagine someone facing significant financial setbacks, such as job loss, unexpected expenses, or overwhelming debt. This situation represents a life struggle that requires navigating financial challenges and rebuilding stability.

Goal Setting and Motivation in Action:

Creating a Budget and Debt Reduction Plan: Goal Setting: The person sets a goal to create a realistic budget to track income and expenses. Additionally, they establish a plan to systematically reduce debt over time. This goal-setting approach provides a clear roadmap for financial recovery.

Setting Employment and Income Goals:

Motivation: To address job loss, the individual sets goals related to employment. This might involve updating their resume, enhancing skills through training, and actively seeking new job opportunities. The motivation comes from the desire to regain financial stability through sustainable income.

Building an Emergency Fund: Goal Setting: Recognizing the importance of financial resilience, the person sets a goal to build an emergency fund. This fund serves as a safety net for unexpected expenses, reducing the impact of future financial shocks. The goal is to achieve a specific savings target over time.

Investing in Financial Education: Motivation: The individual sets a goal to invest time in financial education. This could involve reading books, attending workshops, or seeking advice from financial experts. The motivation is to enhance financial literacy and make informed decisions for long-term financial well-being.

Networking for Career Advancement: Goal Setting: Understanding the value of professional connections, the person sets goals related to networking. This might include attending industry events, joining professional groups, and actively building a network for career advancement. The goal is to create opportunities for improved income and career growth.

Outcome: Through the consistent practice of goal setting and motivation, the individual not only navigates financial setbacks but also experiences improved financial stability and resilience. Achieving goals related to budgeting, debt reduction, employment, emergency funds, and networking contributes to a sense of control over their financial future.

Summary: This example demonstrates how goal setting and motivation can be applied to overcome financial setbacks. By setting specific goals related to budgeting, debt reduction, employment, emergency funds, and networking, individuals can proactively address financial challenges and work towards long-term financial well-being.

Mindfulness and Present Living:

Impact: Struggles can encourage mindfulness. It's like learning to focus on the present moment and appreciate what you have.

Example: Going through a period of stress might lead you to practice mindfulness techniques to stay grounded in the present.

Let's explore an example of mindfulness and present living in the context of life struggles:

Example: Coping with Stress at Work

Life Struggle: Work-related Stress and Overwhelm

Imagine someone facing high levels of stress and overwhelm at work due to tight deadlines, increased responsibilities, and a challenging work environment. This situation represents a life struggle in the professional realm.

Mindfulness and Present Living in Action:

Practicing Mindful Breathing: Mindfulness: The individual incorporates mindfulness into their daily routine, especially during moments of stress. They practice mindful breathing exercises, focusing on each breath to bring their attention to the present moment. This helps create a sense of calm amidst work pressures.

Setting Boundaries and Prioritizing Tasks: Present Living: Instead of constantly worrying about future tasks, the person practices present living by setting boundaries. They break down tasks into manageable steps and prioritize based on what needs immediate attention. This approach helps them stay focused on the current workload.

Engaging in Mindful Breaks:

Mindfulness: Recognizing the importance of breaks, the individual takes mindful breaks throughout the day. These breaks may involve a short walk, stretching exercises, or simply focusing on the sensory experience of a cup of tea. This intentional pause contributes to a more balanced and mindful workday.

Accepting Challenges without Judgment: Present Living: Instead of dwelling on the difficulties, the person practices present living by accepting challenges without judgment. They acknowledge the stressors but refrain from overly identifying with negative emotions. This non-judgmental awareness helps in maintaining mental clarity.

Gratitude Journaling:

Mindfulness: To shift the focus from stressors, the individual engages in gratitude journaling. At the end of each day, they write down things they are grateful for, fostering a mindful awareness of positive aspects even in the midst of challenges.

Outcome: Through the consistent practice of mindfulness and present living, the individual not only copes with work-related stress but also experiences a more balanced and centered approach to their professional challenges. Mindful breathing, setting boundaries, engaging in mindful breaks, accepting challenges without judgment, and gratitude journaling contribute to a healthier work mindset.

Summary: This example illustrates how mindfulness and present living can be applied to cope with work-related stress. By incorporating mindfulness practices into daily routines, setting boundaries, engaging in mindful breaks, accepting challenges without judgment, and cultivating gratitude, individuals can navigate work struggles with a more grounded and present mindset.

Humility and Open-Mindedness: Impact: Life struggles often foster humility. It's like becoming more open-minded and understanding that everyone faces challenges.

Example: Having experienced failure, you might approach success with humility, knowing that setbacks are a part of life.

Let's explore an example of humility and open-mindedness in the context of life struggles:

Example: Career Setbacks and Professional Growth

Life Struggle: Career Setbacks and Challenges

Imagine someone who experiences setbacks in their career, such as not getting a desired promotion, facing a career transition, or encountering obstacles in their professional path. This situation represents a life struggle in the realm of career and personal development.

Humility and Open-Mindedness in Action:

Seeking Feedback with Humility: Humility: Instead of placing blame externally, the individual approaches the situation with humility. They seek feedback from supervisors, colleagues, and mentors to understand areas for improvement. This humility allows them to acknowledge their own shortcomings and areas for growth.

Embracing Constructive Criticism:

Open-Mindedness: Open-mindedness comes into play as the person embraces constructive criticism. Instead of being defensive, they view feedback as an opportunity to learn and grow. This open-minded approach allows them to consider alternative perspectives and adjust their professional approach accordingly.

Exploring New Career Paths:

Humility: Recognizing that career paths may not always follow a linear trajectory, the individual approaches career setbacks with humility. They consider exploring new career paths or acquiring additional skills, acknowledging that there are various routes to professional success.

Networking and Mentorship:

Open-Mindedness: Open-mindedness is demonstrated through the person's willingness to network and seek mentorship. They recognize that learning from others who have navigated similar challenges can provide valuable insights. This open-minded approach allows them to consider different perspectives on career development.

Adapting to Industry Changes:

Humility: In the face of industry changes or technological advancements, the individual approaches the situation with humility. They acknowledge that staying current and adaptable is essential in today's dynamic work environment. This humility allows them to embrace ongoing learning and professional development.

Outcome: Through the consistent practice of humility and open-mindedness, the individual not only navigates career setbacks but also experiences professional growth. Seeking feedback with humility, embracing constructive criticism, exploring new career paths, engaging in networking and mentorship, and adapting to industry changes contribute to a more resilient and open-minded professional mindset.

Summary: This example illustrates how humility and open-mindedness can be applied in the face of career setbacks. By approaching challenges with a humble attitude, seeking feedback, embracing constructive criticism, exploring new paths, engaging in networking, and adapting to changes, individuals can transform setbacks into opportunities for continuous professional growth.

CHAPTER 7
HEALTH

The relationship between health and mindset is complex and bidirectional, meaning that each can influence the other. The impact of health on mindset refers to how physical well-being can affect our mental and emotional states. Here are several ways in which health can influence mindset:

Neurochemical Balance:

Physical health plays a crucial role in maintaining the balance of neurotransmitters in the brain. These neurotransmitters, such as serotonin and dopamine, are essential for regulating mood and emotions. Exercise, a balanced diet, and adequate sleep contribute to the production and regulation of these neurotransmitters, positively influencing our mental state.

Your brain is a complex organ made up of billions of cells called neurons. These neurons communicate with each other through chemicals known as neurotransmitters. Neurotransmitters play a crucial role in regulating your mood, emotions, thoughts, and overall mental well-being.

Neurochemical balance refers to the proper and balanced levels of these neurotransmitters in the brain. When the levels are balanced, your brain functions smoothly, and you feel good both mentally and emotionally. However, imbalances in neurotransmitters can lead to various mental health issues, such as anxiety, depression, or other mood disorders.

Maintaining a healthy neurochemical balance is essential for overall mental well-being, and it can be influenced by factors like genetics, lifestyle, and environmental factors. Strategies such as regular exercise, a balanced diet, sufficient sleep, and stress management can contribute to maintaining a healthy neurochemical balance.

An imbalance in neurochemicals can have various negative effects on our mindset and mental well-being. Neurotransmitters play a crucial role in regulating mood, emotions, and cognitive function. When there's a disruption in the neurochemical balance, it can lead to a range of mental health issues. Here are some negative effects:

Depression:

Imbalances in neurotransmitters, particularly serotonin, have been linked to depression. Low levels of serotonin are associated with feelings of sadness, hopelessness, and a lack of interest or pleasure in activities that were once enjoyable.

Depression can have a profound impact on various aspects of an individual's mindset, affecting thoughts, emotions, behaviors, and overall well-being. Here are some examples of how depression can influence one's mindset:

Negative Thought Patterns:

Individuals experiencing depression often engage in negative thought patterns, such as persistent feelings of worthlessness, self-blame, and pessimism. These thoughts can contribute to a distorted perception of oneself and the world.

Loss of Interest and Pleasure:

A hallmark symptom of depression is anhedonia, which is the reduced ability to experience pleasure or interest in activities that were once enjoyable. This can lead to a sense of emptiness and disconnection from previously satisfying pursuits.

Hopelessness:

Depression can instill a pervasive sense of hopelessness about the future. Individuals may struggle to envision positive outcomes and may feel trapped in a cycle of despair.

Low Self-Esteem:

Depressive thoughts often center around feelings of inadequacy and self-doubt. This can result in a diminished sense of self-worth and a negative self-image.

Fatigue and Lack of Energy:

Physical symptoms of depression, such as fatigue and low energy levels, can contribute to a mindset characterized by lethargy. This can make even simple daily tasks feel overwhelming and exhausting.

Difficulty Concentrating:

Depression can impair cognitive function, making it challenging for individuals to concentrate and make decisions. This can impact work or academic performance and contribute to a sense of frustration.

Sleep Disturbances:

Depression often disrupts sleep patterns, leading to insomnia or excessive sleeping. Poor sleep quality can exacerbate feelings of fatigue and contribute to a negative mindset.

Social Withdrawal:

Depression can lead to social isolation as individuals may withdraw from friends and family. The desire to avoid social interactions can stem from feelings of guilt, shame, or the perception that others won't understand.

Physical Aches and Pains:

Some individuals with depression may experience physical symptoms such as headaches, stomachaches, or muscle pain. These physical manifestations can contribute to a negative mindset and further decrease the motivation to engage in activities.

Suicidal Thoughts:

In severe cases, depression can lead to thoughts of self-harm or suicide. These thoughts are indicative of the extreme emotional pain and despair that individuals with depression may experience.

It's important to recognize that depression is a serious mental health condition, and individuals experiencing symptoms should seek professional help. Psychotherapy, medication, and support from loved ones can play crucial roles in managing and treating depression. If you or someone you know is struggling with depression or suicidal thoughts, it's important to reach out to mental health professionals or helplines for assistance.

HOW TO MANAGE IMPACT OF DEPRESSION

Managing and alleviating the impact of depression on mindset often involves a combination of therapeutic, lifestyle, and sometimes pharmacological interventions. It's important to note that the following suggestions are general in nature, and the most effective approach may vary for each individual. Consulting with a mental health professional is crucial for personalized guidance. Here are some strategies that may help:

Therapy:

Cognitive Behavioral Therapy (CBT): CBT is a widely used therapeutic approach for depression. It helps individuals identify and change negative thought patterns and behaviors, promoting healthier ways of thinking.

Interpersonal Therapy (IPT): IPT focuses on improving interpersonal relationships and communication skills, which can be particularly beneficial for individuals struggling with the social aspects of depression.

Medication: In some cases, antidepressant medications may be prescribed by a psychiatrist to help regulate neurotransmitter levels in the brain. It's important to consult with a healthcare professional to determine the most appropriate medication and dosage.

Lifestyle Changes:

Exercise: Regular physical activity has been shown to have antidepressant effects. Exercise helps release endorphins, which can improve mood and reduce feelings of depression.

Healthy Diet: Nutrient-rich foods can positively impact brain function. Omega-3 fatty acids, for example, found in fish and flaxseeds, have been associated with mood improvement.

Adequate Sleep: Establishing a consistent sleep routine and ensuring sufficient sleep is essential for mental well-being.

Social Support:

Reach out to friends, family, or support groups. Sharing your feelings and experiences with others can provide emotional support and help combat feelings of isolation.

Mindfulness and Meditation:

Practices such as mindfulness meditation and deep breathing exercises can help manage stress and improve overall mental well-being. Mindfulness-based therapies, such as Mindfulness-Based Stress Reduction (MBSR), have been shown to be effective in treating depression.

Set Realistic Goals:

Break down tasks into smaller, more manageable goals. Accomplishing even small goals can provide a sense of achievement and help counter feelings of hopelessness.

Limit Negative Influences:

Identify and reduce exposure to negative influences, whether they be people, situations, or media. Surround yourself with positive and supportive individuals.

Establish Routine:

Creating a daily routine can provide structure and stability, which can be especially helpful during periods of depression.

Professional Help:

Consult with mental health professionals, such as psychologists, counselors, or psychiatrists, who can provide guidance, support, and treatment options.

Monitor and Challenge Negative Thoughts:

Keep a journal to track negative thoughts and challenge them with more balanced and realistic perspectives. This is a key component of cognitive-behavioral approaches.

It's important to remember that overcoming depression is a gradual process, and seeking professional help is a crucial step. If you or someone you know is experiencing depression or having suicidal thoughts, it's important to reach out to mental health professionals or helplines for immediate assistance.Top of Form

Anxiety Disorders:

Neurotransmitter imbalances, including low levels of gamma-aminobutyric acid (GABA) and excessive levels of norepinephrine or glutamate, can contribute to the development of anxiety disorders. This may result in heightened states of worry, fear, and nervousness.

Think of your brain like a control center for your feelings and emotions. It uses messengers called neurotransmitters to send signals between different parts of your brain. When these messengers are in the right amounts, you feel good and balanced.

Now, if there's not enough of a neurotransmitter called gamma-aminobutyric acid (GABA) or too much of others like norepinephrine or glutamate, it can cause problems. Specifically, it might lead to anxiety disorders.

Imagine your brain is like a car. If you have too little brake fluid (GABA) or too much gas (norepinephrine or glutamate), the car might not work right. In your brain, this imbalance can make you feel overly worried, fearful, or nervous - like your mind is stuck in overdrive.

So, keeping these neurotransmitters in the right balance is crucial for a happy and healthy mind.

Causes of Anxiety disorders

Anxiety disorders are mental health conditions characterized by excessive and persistent worry, fear, or nervousness. The impact of neurotransmitter imbalances, particularly involving gamma-aminobutyric acid (GABA), norepinephrine, and glutamate, plays a significant role in the development and maintenance of anxiety disorders. Here's an explanation of how these neurotransmitter imbalances contribute to heightened states of anxiety:

Gamma-Aminobutyric Acid (GABA) Imbalance:

GABA is an inhibitory neurotransmitter that helps regulate the brain's excitability. When GABA levels are low or its function is impaired, it can result in an overactive and hyperexcitable state in the brain. This can lead to heightened anxiety, as the brain struggles to control and inhibit excessive neural activity associated with anxious thoughts and feelings.

Excessive Norepinephrine Levels:

Norepinephrine is a neurotransmitter that plays a role in the body's "fight or flight" response. In individuals with anxiety disorders, there may be an overproduction or insufficient regulation of norepinephrine, leading to an exaggerated stress response. Elevated levels of norepinephrine can contribute to increased heart rate, rapid breathing, and a heightened state of alertness—common symptoms of anxiety.

Glutamate Imbalance:

Glutamate is an excitatory neurotransmitter that facilitates communication between nerve cells. In anxiety disorders, there may be an imbalance in glutamate levels, leading to excessive neural activity and overstimulation. This heightened excitability can contribute to the persistent worry and heightened arousal associated with anxiety.

Hyperactivity in the Amygdala:

The amygdala, a region of the brain involved in processing emotions, is sensitive to neurotransmitter imbalances. An increase in excitatory neurotransmitters (such as glutamate) and a decrease in inhibitory neurotransmitters (such as GABA) can lead to hyperactivity in the amygdala. This hyperactivity is associated with the heightened emotional responses and fear reactions characteristic of anxiety disorders.

Impaired GABAergic Inhibition:

GABAergic inhibition is a process by which GABA inhibits the activity of certain neurons, calming the central nervous system. When there is an imbalance, the inhibitory effects of GABA may be impaired, contributing to an inability to regulate and control excessive neural activity associated with anxiety.

Imagine your brain is like a busy traffic intersection, and there are signals telling the cars (which are messages in your brain) when to stop and when to go. GABA (gamma-aminobutyric acid) is like the traffic cop that says, "Hey, slow down or stop!" It's a calming messenger in your brain.

When there's enough GABA around, it helps to keep things chill and balanced. It's like having a good traffic cop at the intersection, making sure everything flows smoothly and preventing chaos.

So, GABA is a brain chemical that helps to put the brakes on excessive activity in your brain, making you feel calm and relaxed. When you're feeling stressed or anxious, having enough GABA is like having a calm and collected traffic cop helping to ease the mental traffic.

Feedback Loop of Anxiety:

Neurotransmitter imbalances can contribute to a feedback loop, where heightened anxiety leads to further imbalances, perpetuating the cycle of anxious thoughts and feelings. This can contribute to the chronic and self-reinforcing nature of anxiety disorders.

Understanding the role of neurotransmitter imbalances in anxiety disorders is essential for developing effective treatment strategies. Medications targeting these neurotransmitters, such as selective serotonin reuptake inhibitors (SSRIs) or benzodiazepines, are commonly prescribed to help regulate neurotransmitter levels and alleviate symptoms of anxiety. Additionally, psychotherapy, particularly cognitive-behavioral therapy (CBT), can be effective in addressing the cognitive and behavioral aspects of anxiety disorders. It's important for individuals experiencing symptoms of anxiety to seek professional help for an accurate diagnosis and tailored treatment plan.

Mood Swings:

Fluctuations in neurotransmitter levels, such as dopamine and serotonin, can lead to mood swings. These sudden changes in mood may range from irritability and frustration to elation and euphoria.

Impaired Cognitive Function:

Neurotransmitter imbalances can negatively impact cognitive functions such as memory, attention, and concentration. This can affect academic or work performance and lead to difficulties in problem-solving and decision-making.

Sleep Disturbances:

Neurotransmitter imbalances, especially involving melatonin and serotonin, can disrupt sleep patterns. This may lead to insomnia, difficulty falling asleep or staying asleep, and poor overall sleep quality.

Impulsivity and Risk-Taking Behavior:

Imbalances in neurotransmitters like dopamine can contribute to impulsive behavior and an increased inclination toward risk-taking. This can have consequences in various aspects of life, including personal relationships and work.

Decreased Motivation:

Low levels of dopamine, a neurotransmitter associated with motivation and reward, can result in decreased motivation and anhedonia—a reduced ability to experience pleasure from activities that were once enjoyable.

Eating Disorders:

Neurotransmitter imbalances, particularly involving serotonin, have been implicated in eating disorders such as bulimia and anorexia nervosa. These conditions are often associated with distorted body image and unhealthy eating habits.

Substance Abuse:

Imbalances in neurotransmitters, particularly dopamine, are linked to the reward system in the brain. Some individuals may turn to substance abuse as a way to artificially stimulate neurotransmitter release, leading to a cycle of dependence and addiction.

It's important to note that the relationship between neurochemical balance and mental health is complex, and individual responses can vary. Mental health conditions are influenced by a combination of genetic, environmental, and biological factors. Seeking professional help, such as from a mental health professional or psychiatrist, is crucial for accurately diagnosing and addressing neurochemical imbalances and their associated negative effects on mindset.

STRESS MANAGEMENT

Cognitive Function:

Good health is essential for optimal cognitive function. Physical well-being, including cardiovascular health, affects blood flow to the brain, which in turn influences cognitive abilities such as memory, attention, and problem-solving. When the body is healthy, the brain is more likely to function at its best.

Stress Management:

Chronic health issues or persistent pain can contribute to stress, which has a direct impact on mindset. Stress hormones like cortisol can affect mood, increase anxiety, and contribute to feelings of overwhelm. Conversely, engaging in stress-reducing activities, such as exercise or relaxation techniques, can improve health and positively impact mindset.

Self-Esteem and Body Image:

Physical health can influence how we perceive ourselves. Chronic health conditions or body image concerns can contribute to low self-esteem and negative self-perception. Conversely, engaging in activities that promote physical well-being can boost self-esteem and positively influence body image, leading to a more positive mindset.

Energy Levels and Motivation:

Physical health is closely tied to energy levels and motivation. When the body is healthy, individuals are more likely to have the energy and motivation needed to engage in activities, pursue goals, and maintain a positive outlook on life. Conversely, poor health can lead to fatigue, lethargy, and a lack of motivation.

Social Interactions:

Health can impact our ability to engage in social activities. Chronic health issues may limit one's ability to participate in social events, leading to feelings of isolation and loneliness. Positive social interactions, on the other hand, can contribute to emotional well-being and a positive mindset.

Resilience to Challenges:

Good physical health can enhance resilience in the face of life's challenges. When the body is strong and healthy, individuals are better equipped to cope with stress and adversity. Conversely, poor health may make it more difficult to bounce back from setbacks, potentially leading to a more negative mindset.

Summary, the impact of health on mindset is multi-faceted and interconnected. Taking care of one's physical well-being through healthy lifestyle choices, regular exercise, and proper medical care can contribute to a positive mindset, while neglecting health may lead to negative effects on mental and emotional well-being.

CHAPTER 8
IMPACT OF MOTIVATION ON OUR MINDSET

Motivation refers to the internal or external factors that drive, direct, and sustain an individual's behavior towards a particular goal or outcome. It involves the activation of psychological and physiological processes that energize and guide an individual's actions, effort, and persistence. Motivation can be influenced by a variety of factors, including personal goals, values, expectations, desires, rewards, and external stimuli.

In essence, motivation is what prompts a person to take action, make an effort, and persevere in the pursuit of a desired outcome. It plays a crucial role in goal-setting, decision-making, and overall behavior, influencing the direction and intensity of human activities. Motivation can be intrinsic, stemming from internal desires and personal values, or extrinsic, driven by external rewards or avoidance of negative consequences. Understanding and harnessing motivation is key to personal development, achievement, and sustained effort in various aspects of life.Impact of

The impact of motive on our mindset is significant and multifaceted. Motives, or the underlying reasons that drive our actions, play a crucial role in shaping our thoughts, behaviors, and overall mindset. Here are some ways in which motives can influence our mindset:

Direction and Focus:

Motives provide a sense of direction and purpose. They guide our thoughts and actions toward specific goals or outcomes.

A clear and positive motive can help focus our mindset on constructive and productive thoughts, fostering a sense of purpose and motivation.

Emotional Tone:

Motives can influence the emotional tone of our mindset. Positive motives often lead to positive emotions, while negative motives can contribute to negative emotions.

For example, a motive driven by a desire to help others may generate feelings of empathy and satisfaction, contributing to a positive mindset.

Perception and Interpretation:

Motives can shape how we perceive and interpret events and information. They act as a filter through which we view the world.

A person with a motive for personal growth may see challenges as opportunities for learning, while someone with a fear-based motive may interpret the same challenges as threats.

Resilience and Persistence:

The strength of our motives can impact our resilience and persistence in the face of challenges. Strong, intrinsic motives are often associated with greater perseverance.

When faced with setbacks, individuals with a strong motive may be more likely to maintain a positive and determined mindset, seeing challenges as temporary obstacles.

Decision-Making:

Motives influence decision-making processes. Our choices are often aligned with our underlying motives, consciously or unconsciously.

Understanding our motives can lead to more intentional decision-making, contributing to a mindset that is in harmony with our values and goals.

Relationships:

Motives can shape the nature of our relationships. Whether our motives are collaborative, competitive, or cooperative can influence our interactions with others.

A shared motive within a group can contribute to a collective mindset that fosters collaboration and unity.

Personal Growth:

Motives are integral to personal growth. A mindset focused on self-improvement is often fueled by motives related to learning, development, and achievement.

Regularly reassessing and aligning motives with personal values can contribute to ongoing positive mindset development.

Summary, motives serve as a powerful force that shapes our mindset by influencing our thoughts, emotions, behaviors, and overall perspective on life. Being aware of our motives and ensuring they align with our values can contribute to a more intentional and positive mindset.

NEGATIVE IMPACT OF MOTIVATION

While motivation generally has a positive influence on mindset, it's important to recognize that not all motivations lead to beneficial outcomes. Here are some potential negative impacts of motivation on mindset:

Unhealthy Competition:

Motivation driven solely by a desire to outperform others can lead to unhealthy competition and comparison. This may result in stress, anxiety, and a mindset focused on winning at the expense of collaboration.

External Validation:

Seeking external validation as a primary motivation can contribute to a mindset that is overly dependent on others' opinions. This may lead to feelings of inadequacy or a constant need for approval.

Fear-Based Motivation:

Motivation rooted in fear, such as fear of failure or rejection, can lead to a mindset characterized by anxiety and avoidance. This fear-based mindset may hinder creativity and risk-taking.

Burnout:

Overemphasis on achieving goals without considering well-being can lead to burnout. A mindset driven by relentless motivation to succeed may neglect self-care and work-life balance, resulting in exhaustion and negative consequences for mental health.

Short-Term Focus:

Motivations that are solely focused on short-term gains may lead to a mindset that overlooks long-term consequences. This can result in impulsive decision-making and a lack of consideration for sustainable success.

Lack of Intrinsic Motivation:

Relying too heavily on external rewards or punishments can diminish intrinsic motivation. If the primary motivation is external, such as financial incentives, the mindset may become transactional rather than driven by genuine passion or interest.

Narrow Perspective:

A singular, intense motivation can sometimes lead to tunnel vision, where individuals become fixated on a specific goal to the detriment of other important aspects of life. This can limit personal growth and overall well-being.

Impaired Relationships:

Motivations that prioritize individual success over collaboration may negatively impact relationships. This can lead to a mindset that values personal gain at the expense of teamwork and mutual support.

Perfectionism:

Excessive motivation for perfection can result in a mindset characterized by unrealistic standards and a fear of making mistakes. This mindset may hinder creativity and risk-taking, as individuals may avoid challenges to avoid failure.

Lack of Adaptability:

Overly rigid motivations may lead to a mindset that is resistant to change. In a rapidly evolving world, adaptability is crucial, and motivations that resist change can hinder personal and professional development.

It's important for individuals to reflect on their motivations regularly, ensuring they align with their values and contribute to a positive and balanced mindset. Striking a balance between motivation and well-being is essential for long-term success and fulfillment.

How to remove negative impact of Motivation mindset

If you recognize that the motivation, you're experiencing is having a negative impact on your mindset, there are several strategies you can employ to mitigate these effects and foster a more positive and balanced mindset. Here are some suggestions:

Self-Reflection:

Take time to reflect on your motivations. Understand the underlying reasons for your goals and assess whether they align with your values and well-being.

Set Realistic Goals:

Break down your goals into smaller, more manageable tasks. Setting realistic and achievable goals can reduce feelings of overwhelm and make the journey more sustainable.

Cultivate Intrinsic Motivation:

Identify aspects of your goals that genuinely interest and motivate you. Cultivate a sense of intrinsic motivation by focusing on the joy of the process, learning, and personal growth.

Emphasize Learning Over Perfection:

Shift your mindset from a focus on perfection to one that values learning and improvement. Understand that making mistakes is a natural part of growth.

Practice Mindfulness:

Engage in mindfulness practices such as meditation or deep breathing exercises. These practices can help you stay present, reduce stress, and gain clarity on your motivations.

Diversify Motivations:

Balance your motivations by incorporating a variety of factors, such as personal fulfilment, collaboration, and well-being. Avoid fixating on a single source of motivation.

Seek Social Support:

Share your goals and motivations with friends, family, or mentors. Having a support system can provide valuable perspectives and encouragement, helping to counteract negative effects.

Celebrate Progress:

Acknowledge and celebrate your achievements along the way, no matter how small. Recognizing progress can boost your motivation and contribute to a positive mindset.

Establish Boundaries:

Set clear boundaries to prevent burnout. Ensure a balance between work, personal life, and self-care. Recognize the importance of rest and relaxation in maintaining a healthy mindset.

Reassess and Adjust:

Regularly reassess your motivations and goals. Be willing to adjust them if they no longer align with your values or if they are contributing to negative effects on your mindset.

Focus on Well-Being:

Prioritize your mental and physical well-being. Ensure that your motivations contribute to a holistic sense of health and happiness rather than causing stress or harm.

Professional Help:

If negative impacts persist, consider seeking guidance from a mental health professional. They can provide valuable insights and strategies to address the underlying issues.

Remember that motivation and mindset are interconnected, and fostering a positive mindset often involves aligning your motivations with your overall well-being and values. Regular self-reflection and adjustments to your approach can contribute to a healthier and more sustainable motivational mindset.

CHAPTER 9
WILL POWER

Willpower refers to the mental strength and self-discipline that enables individuals to control their actions, resist temptations, and persevere in the pursuit of long-term goals. It involves the ability to make conscious choices, often sacrificing immediate gratification for the sake of achieving more significant, future outcomes. Willpower is essential for self-regulation, decision-making, and maintaining focus in the face of challenges. It is considered a cognitive resource that individuals can cultivate and strengthen through practice and effort. Strong willpower is associated with the capacity to overcome obstacles, adhere to personal values, and sustain motivation in various aspects of life.

Willpower, often described as the ability to exert self-control and resist short-term temptations for the sake of long-term goals, can have a significant impact on our mindset. Here are some ways in which willpower influences the mind:

Goal Achievement:

Willpower is crucial for setting and achieving goals. It helps individuals stay focused on their objectives, resist distractions, and overcome obstacles that may arise during the pursuit of those goals.

Resilience in the Face of Challenges:

A strong willpower enables individuals to persevere through difficulties and setbacks. It contributes to a resilient mindset, allowing individuals to bounce back from failures and maintain a positive outlook.

Delayed Gratification:

Willpower plays a key role in delaying immediate gratification for long-term rewards. This ability to resist instant rewards in favor of more significant, future benefits is associated with a mindset geared toward sustained success.

Decision-Making:

Willpower helps in making better decisions by resisting impulsive choices. It allows individuals to think more rationally and consider the long-term consequences of their actions, contributing to a thoughtful and strategic mindset.

Self-Discipline:

Willpower is closely tied to self-discipline. It enables individuals to regulate their behavior, adhere to routines, and make choices that align with their values. This disciplined mindset fosters personal growth and development.

Stress Management:

Individuals with strong willpower may be better equipped to manage stress. The ability to stay focused on goals and resist succumbing to stressors can contribute to a more positive and adaptive mindset.

Building Habits:

Willpower is instrumental in establishing and maintaining positive habits. It allows individuals to initiate and sustain behavior changes, contributing to a mindset oriented toward continuous improvement.

Increased Confidence:

Successfully exercising willpower in the face of challenges can boost self-confidence. This increased confidence can shape a positive mindset, reinforcing the belief that one has the capacity to overcome difficulties.

Mindfulness and Awareness:

Willpower is associated with mindfulness, the ability to be present and aware of one's thoughts and actions. This heightened awareness contributes to a more intentional and focused mindset.

Balancing Short-Term and Long-Term Goals:

Willpower helps individuals strike a balance between short-term desires and long-term goals. This balance is crucial for maintaining a mindset that considers both immediate gratification and future success.

Enhanced Mental Toughness:

Willpower contributes to mental toughness, the ability to persevere and maintain performance under pressure. This mental toughness positively influences mindset, particularly in challenging situations.

Cultivating and strengthening willpower can have lasting effects on mindset, empowering individuals to navigate challenges, pursue goals, and foster a positive and goal-oriented outlook on life. It's important to note that willpower, like a muscle, can be developed and strengthened through practice and conscious effort.

NEGATIVE IMPACT OF WILLPOWER

While willpower is generally considered a positive and valuable trait, there can be potential negative impacts if it is excessively rigid or if individuals experience what is known as "ego depletion." Here are a few potential negative aspects:

Ego Depletion:

Ego depletion is a concept that suggests self-control and willpower draw from a limited pool of mental resources. If individuals exert intense willpower in one area, they may experience a temporary depletion of these resources, leading to reduced self-control in other areas. This can result in a negative impact on mindset as individuals may feel fatigued or demotivated.

Stress and Burnout:

Constantly relying on willpower without allowing for breaks or self-care can contribute to chronic stress and burnout. This may lead to a negative mindset characterized by fatigue, frustration, and a sense of being overwhelmed.

Perfectionism:

Excessive willpower can sometimes manifest as perfectionism, where individuals set unrealistically high standards for themselves. This perfectionistic mindset may contribute to feelings of inadequacy, frustration, and a fear of failure.

Rigidity:

Overemphasis on willpower may result in a rigid mindset, where individuals become resistant to flexibility or adapting to changing circumstances. This inflexibility can hinder problem-solving and creativity.

Neglect of Well-Being:

Individuals with a strong willpower may push themselves too hard, neglecting important aspects of their well-being such as rest, relaxation, and social connections. This neglect can lead to a negative mindset and impact overall life satisfaction.

Social Isolation:

Excessive willpower may lead individuals to prioritize personal goals over social connections. This could contribute to social isolation and a mindset focused solely on individual achievement at the expense of meaningful relationships.

Guilt and Self-Criticism:

If individuals perceive a lack of willpower in certain areas, they may experience guilt and self-criticism. This negative self-talk can contribute to a mindset that undermines self-esteem and overall well-being.

It's important to note that the negative impacts mentioned above are often associated with an imbalance in how willpower is applied or a lack of self-compassion. Striking a balance, practicing self-care, and being mindful of the potential limitations of willpower can help mitigate these negative effects. Building a mindset that recognizes the importance of balance, adaptability, and self-compassion can contribute to overall well-being.

HOW TO REMOVE NEGATIVE IMPACT OF WILL POWER

To mitigate the negative impacts of willpower on your mindset, consider adopting a more balanced and mindful approach. Here are some strategies to help remove or reduce the negative effects:

Practice Self-Compassion:

Be kind to yourself and recognize that everyone has limits. Avoid harsh self-criticism, and instead, practice self-compassion when facing challenges or setbacks.

Set Realistic Goals:

Establish achievable and realistic goals. Break larger goals into smaller, more manageable tasks to avoid feeling overwhelmed and reduce the likelihood of burnout.

Prioritize Well-Being:

Place importance on your overall well-being, including physical and mental health. Ensure you are getting adequate rest, nutrition, and exercise to support your energy levels and resilience.

Embrace Flexibility:

Be open to adjusting your plans and goals based on changing circumstances. Embrace flexibility and recognize that adaptability is a valuable trait for a healthy mindset.

Mindfulness and Mindful Breathing:

Incorporate mindfulness practices into your routine. Mindful breathing and meditation can help you stay present, reduce stress, and maintain focus without depleting your mental resources.

Take Breaks:

Allow yourself breaks and moments of relaxation. Stepping away from tasks, even for a short time, can rejuvenate your mental energy and prevent burnout.

Build Support Systems:

Surround yourself with supportive friends, family, or mentors. Sharing your goals and challenges with others can provide valuable perspectives and encouragement.

Celebrate Small Wins:

Acknowledge and celebrate your achievements, no matter how small. Recognizing progress can boost motivation and contribute to a more positive mindset.

Mind-Body Practices:

Engage in activities that promote a connection between the mind and body, such as yoga or tai chi. These practices can help integrate mental and physical well-being.

Reflect on Values:

Regularly reflect on your core values and ensure that your goals align with them. This alignment can provide a sense of purpose and motivation without the negative impact of willpower.

Set Boundaries:

Establish clear boundaries to prevent overexertion. Recognize the importance of balance in your life, separating work and personal time to maintain a healthy mindset.

Seek Professional Guidance:

If negative impacts persist, consider seeking guidance from a mental health professional. They can provide personalized strategies and support to help you navigate challenges and improve your mindset.

Remember that willpower is a valuable resource, but it should be used judiciously and in balance with other aspects of your life. By fostering self-compassion, setting realistic goals, and prioritizing well-being, you can remove or reduce the negative impact of willpower on your mindset.

CHAPTER 10
INTELLIGENCE

Intelligence is a complex and multifaceted trait that encompasses the ability to acquire, understand, apply knowledge, and adapt to new situations effectively. It involves the capacity to reason, solve problems, learn from experience, comprehend complex ideas, think abstractly, and learn quickly. Intelligence is not limited to academic or cognitive abilities but also includes practical, social, and emotional competencies.

There are various theories of intelligence, and different perspectives exist on how to define and measure it. Traditional views often focused on cognitive abilities such as logical reasoning and memory, while contemporary perspectives, such as Howard Gardner's theory of multiple intelligences, acknowledge diverse forms of intelligence, including interpersonal, intrapersonal, spatial, musical, and more.

In essence, intelligence reflects an individual's overall mental capability and adaptive functioning across a range of contexts. It is a dynamic and evolving trait influenced by genetic factors, environmental stimuli, and life experiences.

Intelligence can have a profound impact on our mindset, influencing the way we perceive, understand, and navigate the world. Here are some key ways in which intelligence can shape our mindset:

Cognitive Abilities:

Intelligence is often associated with cognitive abilities such as problem-solving, critical thinking, and decision-making. A higher level of intelligence can contribute to a mindset that is analytical, strategic, and adept at processing information.

Learning and Adaptability:

Intelligent individuals tend to be more effective learners. A mindset influenced by intelligence is often characterized by curiosity, a love of learning, and adaptability in the face of new information and challenges.

Complex Thinking:

Higher intelligence is linked to the ability to engage in complex and abstract thinking. This can impact mindset by fostering a comfort with ambiguity, an appreciation for nuance, and the capacity to consider multiple perspectives.

Problem-Solving Skills:

Intelligent individuals often excel in problem-solving. Their mindset is inclined towards viewing challenges as opportunities for solutions, leading to a positive and proactive approach to obstacles.

Innovation and Creativity:

Intelligence is associated with creativity and innovative thinking. A mindset influenced by intelligence may be more open to unconventional ideas, experimentation, and creative problem-solving.

Emotional Intelligence:

Intelligence extends beyond cognitive abilities to include emotional intelligence. A high level of emotional intelligence can contribute to a mindset characterized by empathy, effective interpersonal relationships, and a nuanced understanding of one's own emotions.

Self-Reflection:

Intelligent individuals often engage in reflective thinking about themselves and the world around them. This self-awareness can shape a mindset that is attuned to personal strengths, weaknesses, and areas for growth.

Goal Orientation:

Intelligence can contribute to a mindset focused on setting and achieving goals. Intelligent individuals may be more likely to approach challenges with a strategic plan, persistence, and a long-term perspective.

Open-Mindedness:

Higher intelligence is associated with open-mindedness and a willingness to consider diverse viewpoints. This can influence a mindset that is adaptable, receptive to new ideas, and capable of adjusting perspectives based on evidence.

Resilience:

Intelligence is linked to resilience in the face of adversity. A mindset influenced by intelligence may be more resilient, bouncing back from setbacks with a positive and forward-looking attitude.

Global Awareness:

Intelligent individuals often have a broader awareness of global issues and a capacity to understand complex, interconnected systems. This global perspective can shape a mindset that is socially conscious and globally oriented.

Continuous Learning:

Intelligence is often associated with a love for learning that extends beyond formal education. A mindset influenced by intelligence may be characterized by a lifelong commitment to acquiring new knowledge and skills.

It's important to note that intelligence is a multifaceted trait, and its impact on mindset can vary among individuals. Additionally, mindset is influenced by a combination of factors, including experiences, values, and personality. While intelligence can contribute positively to mindset, other qualities such as emotional intelligence, resilience, and adaptability also play crucial roles in shaping how individuals approach life's challenges.

Negative Impact of Intelligence

While intelligence is generally considered a positive trait, it can potentially have some negative impacts on mindset, depending on how it is expressed or experienced. Here are a few potential drawbacks or challenges associated with high intelligence:

Overthinking:

Intelligent individuals may be prone to overanalyzing situations, leading to excessive rumination and worry. This tendency can contribute to stress and anxiety, impacting overall well-being and mindset.

Perfectionism:

High intelligence can be associated with perfectionistic tendencies, where individuals set unrealistically high standards for themselves. This perfectionism may lead to chronic dissatisfaction, self-criticism, and a negative mindset.

Social Challenges:

Extremely high intelligence may lead to challenges in social interactions. Individuals with significantly higher intellectual abilities may find it challenging to relate to others on a similar intellectual level, potentially leading to feelings of isolation or difficulty in forming close relationships.

Imposter Syndrome:

Intelligent individuals may experience imposter syndrome, a phenomenon where they doubt their accomplishments and fear being exposed as a fraud. This can contribute to feelings of insecurity and negatively impact mindset.

Intolerance of Others:

In some cases, high intelligence may lead to impatience or intolerance with individuals who do not share similar cognitive abilities or perspectives. This lack of patience can strain relationships and contribute to a negative mindset.

Existential Concerns:

Extremely intelligent individuals may grapple with existential questions or a heightened awareness of the complexities of life. This existential thinking can lead to feelings of existential anxiety and may impact overall outlook and mindset.

Difficulty in Finding Challenges:

Highly intelligent individuals may struggle to find challenges that engage and stimulate their minds, leading to boredom and a sense of unfulfillment. This lack of stimulation can contribute to a negative mindset.

High Sensitivity:

Intelligence may be associated with heightened sensitivity, both emotionally and intellectually. This sensitivity can make individuals more susceptible to stressors and negative emotions, influencing their overall mindset.

Difficulty in Accepting Criticism:

Intelligent individuals may find it challenging to accept criticism, as they may place a high value on their intellectual abilities. Difficulty in receiving constructive feedback can hinder personal and professional growth and impact mindset.

Overestimation of Abilities:

Extremely intelligent individuals may overestimate their abilities, leading to a sense of arrogance or a lack of humility. This overestimation can hinder collaboration and contribute to a negative mindset in social and professional contexts.

It's important to note that these potential negative impacts are not universal and may not apply to all individuals with high intelligence.

Additionally, many of these challenges can be mitigated through self-awareness, emotional intelligence, and the development of coping strategies. The key is to foster a balanced and healthy mindset that considers the social and emotional aspects of intelligence alongside cognitive abilities.

HOW TO REMOVE NEGATIVE IMPACT OF INTELLIGENCE

If you find that your high intelligence is having a negative impact on your mindset, there are several strategies you can employ to mitigate these effects and foster a healthier and more balanced mindset:

Cultivate Humility:

Practice humility by acknowledging that intelligence is just one aspect of a person, and everyone has unique strengths and weaknesses. Embrace a mindset that values diversity of abilities and perspectives.

Develop Emotional Intelligence:

Focus on developing emotional intelligence to better understand and manage your own emotions, as well as those of others. This can enhance your interpersonal skills and contribute to more positive relationships.

Set Realistic Expectations:

Establish realistic expectations for yourself and others. Recognize that perfection is unattainable, and allow room for mistakes and learning experiences. Set achievable goals that promote growth without undue pressure.

Practice Mindfulness:

Engage in mindfulness practices to stay present and reduce overthinking. Mindfulness can help you manage stress, increase self-awareness, and promote a more balanced mindset.

Seek Social Connection:

Foster meaningful social connections with a diverse group of people. This can provide a broader perspective, reduce feelings of isolation, and contribute to a more positive mindset.

Challenge Perfectionism:

Challenge perfectionistic tendencies by reframing mistakes as opportunities for learning and growth. Celebrate progress and effort rather than focusing solely on outcomes.

Embrace a Growth Mindset:

Adopt a growth mindset, which involves seeing challenges as opportunities to learn and improve. Embrace the idea that abilities can be developed through dedication and effort.

Find Intellectual Challenges:

Seek out intellectual challenges that engage and stimulate your mind. This can help alleviate boredom and contribute to a more fulfilling and positive mindset.

Accept Constructive Criticism:

Develop the ability to accept constructive criticism with an open mind. View feedback as a valuable tool for personal and professional development, rather than a threat to your intelligence.

Engage in Hobbies and Interests:

Pursue hobbies and interests outside of your intellectual pursuits. This can provide balance, relaxation, and a sense of accomplishment in areas beyond cognitive abilities.

Practice Gratitude:

Cultivate gratitude by focusing on the positive aspects of your life and acknowledging the contributions of others. This can shift your mindset toward a more optimistic and appreciative perspective.

Seek Professional Support:

If negative impacts persist or become overwhelming, consider seeking support from a mental health professional. They can provide guidance and strategies tailored to your specific needs.

Remember that intelligence is a multifaceted trait, and everyone faces challenges. By adopting these strategies, you can work towards a mindset that is more balanced, resilient, and conducive to overall well-being.

CHAPTER 11
REASONING

Reasoning is the cognitive process of thinking systematically, logically, and analytically to make sense of information, solve problems, draw conclusions, and make informed decisions. It involves the ability to assess evidence, evaluate arguments, and reach logical conclusions based on sound judgment. Reasoning encompasses various forms, including deductive reasoning (drawing specific conclusions from general principles), inductive reasoning (forming generalizations based on specific observations), and abductive reasoning (making educated guesses or hypotheses to explain observations).

In essence, reasoning is a mental activity that involves making connections between pieces of information, understanding relationships, and applying logic to arrive at conclusions or solutions. It is a fundamental cognitive skill that plays a crucial role in critical thinking, problem-solving, and decision-making across different domains.

Reasoning plays a crucial role in shaping our mindset, influencing the way we think, make decisions, and approach various aspects of life. Here are some key impacts of reasoning on our mindset:

Critical Thinking:

Reasoning is fundamental to critical thinking, allowing individuals to analyze information, evaluate arguments, and make informed judgments. A mindset shaped by strong reasoning skills tends to be more analytical and discerning.

Problem-Solving:

Reasoning is essential for effective problem-solving. A mindset grounded in strong reasoning abilities is likely to approach challenges with a systematic and logical approach, seeking solutions through thoughtful analysis.

Logical Decision-Making:

Reasoning influences logical decision-making processes. Individuals with a mindset guided by sound reasoning are more likely to make decisions based on evidence, coherence, and a rational assessment of available options.

Understanding Cause and Effect:

Reasoning helps individuals understand cause-and-effect relationships. A mindset influenced by reasoning is attuned to the consequences of actions, fostering a more thoughtful and strategic approach to decision-making.

Open-Mindedness:

Strong reasoning skills can contribute to open-mindedness. A mindset grounded in reasoning is more likely to consider alternative perspectives, entertain new ideas, and adapt beliefs based on evidence and sound arguments.

Effective Communication:

Reasoning is integral to effective communication. Individuals with a mindset influenced by strong reasoning can articulate their thoughts clearly, construct persuasive arguments, and engage in meaningful discussions.

Conflict Resolution:

Reasoning contributes to effective conflict resolution. A mindset shaped by reasoning skills is better equipped to understand different viewpoints, identify common ground, and find mutually acceptable solutions.

Learning and Adaptability:

Reasoning is essential for learning and adaptability. A mindset influenced by strong reasoning skills is more receptive to new information, facilitating continuous learning and adaptability in various situations.

Risk Assessment:

Reasoning plays a role in evaluating risks and benefits. A mindset guided by reasoning is more likely to assess potential risks and make decisions that balance the potential outcomes in a thoughtful manner.

Reduction of Cognitive Biases:

Reasoning helps individuals identify and mitigate cognitive biases. A mindset influenced by strong reasoning is better equipped to recognize and address biases, leading to more objective and rational decision-making.

Ethical Considerations:

Reasoning is crucial in ethical decision-making. A mindset shaped by reasoning skills is more likely to consider ethical implications, moral principles, and societal values in decision-making processes.

Scientific Thinking:

Reasoning is foundational to scientific thinking. A mindset influenced by reasoning skills is more likely to adopt a scientific approach, emphasizing empirical evidence, experimentation, and logical deduction.

Summary, reasoning significantly influences the way we approach problems, make decisions, and interact with the world. A mindset enriched by strong reasoning skills tends to be more analytical, adaptable, and capable of making well-informed choices in various aspects of life.

Negative Impact of Reasoning

While reasoning is generally a valuable and positive cognitive skill, there are certain situations where it might have negative impacts on our mindset. Here are a few potential drawbacks or challenges associated with reasoning:

Overthinking:

Excessive reasoning can lead to overthinking, where individuals dwell on details, possibilities, and potential outcomes. This can result in analysis paralysis, stress, and a tendency to magnify problems.

Perfectionism:

Strong reasoning skills may contribute to perfectionistic tendencies, where individuals set unrealistically high standards for themselves. This perfectionism can lead to chronic dissatisfaction, self-criticism, and a negative mindset.

Cynicism:

Overreliance on reasoning without considering emotional or social factors may lead to cynicism. This overly skeptical mindset can impact trust in relationships and contribute to a negative outlook on people and situations.

Lack of Emotional Connection:

Individuals who heavily rely on reasoning may struggle with expressing or understanding emotions. This can result in a lack of emotional connection with others, potentially leading to feelings of isolation.

Difficulty in Decision-Making:

Overthinking and excessive consideration of possibilities can make decision-making challenging. Individuals may become indecisive or overly cautious, fearing making the wrong choice.

Rigidity:

Excessive reliance on reasoning alone may lead to a rigid mindset, where individuals are unwilling to consider alternative perspectives or adapt their beliefs. This inflexibility can hinder personal and intellectual growth.

Analysis Paralysis:

Analysis paralysis occurs when individuals are overwhelmed by the need to consider every detail before making a decision. This can result in delayed decision-making and missed opportunities.

Conflict in Relationships:

An overly logical mindset may lead to communication challenges in relationships. Emotional nuances may be overlooked, and individuals may struggle to connect with others on a more empathetic level.

Loss of Intuition:

Overemphasis on reasoning might lead to a devaluation of intuition or gut feelings. Ignoring these intuitive signals can result in missed opportunities or a failure to consider important emotional aspects of a situation.

Inability to Accept Uncertainty:

Some individuals who heavily rely on reasoning may find it challenging to accept uncertainty. This fear of the unknown can contribute to anxiety and a negative mindset.

It's important to note that these potential negative impacts are not inherent to reasoning itself but rather arise from imbalances or extremes in how reasoning is applied. Achieving a healthy and balanced mindset involves integrating reasoning with emotional intelligence, flexibility, and an understanding of the social context. Striking a balance between analytical thinking and recognizing the value of emotions and intuition can contribute to a more well-rounded and positive mindset.

Mitigate negative impact of reasoning

If you find that the negative impact of reasoning is affecting your mindset, there are several strategies you can adopt to mitigate these effects and foster a more balanced and positive outlook:

Practice Mindfulness:

Engage in mindfulness practices to bring awareness to your thoughts without judgment. Mindfulness can help you observe negative thought patterns related to overthinking and reasoning, allowing you to let go of unhelpful ideas.

Set Realistic Standards:

Acknowledge that perfection is unattainable. Set realistic standards for yourself and be compassionate when you fall short. Understand that mistakes and imperfections are part of the learning process.

Embrace Emotional Intelligence:

Develop emotional intelligence by paying attention to your own emotions and the emotions of others. Recognize that emotions play a crucial role in decision-making and interpersonal relationships.

Limit Overthinking:

Set time limits for decision-making and problem-solving to avoid excessive overthinking. When a decision needs to be made, allow yourself a reasonable amount of time, and then commit to a choice.

Cultivate Flexibility:

Practice flexibility in your thinking. Be open to considering alternative viewpoints, adapting to new information, and adjusting your beliefs when necessary. Embrace a growth mindset that values learning and development.

Balance Reasoning with Intuition:

Recognize the value of intuition and gut feelings. Allow yourself to consider not only logical reasoning but also your instincts and feelings when making decisions or assessing situations.

Focus on Solutions:

Instead of dwelling on problems, shift your focus to finding solutions. Channel your reasoning abilities into constructive problem-solving rather than getting caught up in negative or overwhelming thoughts.

Build Self-Compassion:

Cultivate self-compassion by treating yourself with the same kindness and understanding that you would offer to a friend. Acknowledge that everyone makes mistakes, and it's okay not to have all the answers.

Seek Support:

Share your thoughts and concerns with friends, family, or a trusted mentor. Discussing your reasoning process with others can provide different perspectives and help alleviate feelings of isolation.

Engage in Relaxation Techniques:

Incorporate relaxation techniques, such as deep breathing exercises or meditation, to manage stress and anxiety associated with negative thought patterns. These practices can promote a calmer and more centered mindset.

Challenge Negative Thoughts:

Actively challenge negative thoughts related to reasoning. Ask yourself if these thoughts are based on evidence, if they are helpful, and if there are alternative, more positive perspectives.

Professional Help:

If negative thought patterns persist and significantly impact your well-being, consider seeking support from a mental health professional. They can provide guidance and strategies tailored to your specific situation.

Remember that achieving a balanced mindset is an ongoing process, and it's okay to seek support when needed. By incorporating these strategies, you can work towards mitigating the negative impact of reasoning and fostering a more positive and adaptive mindset.

CHAPTER 12
PERCEPTION

Perception refers to the process by which individuals interpret and make sense of sensory information from their environment. It involves the organization, identification, and interpretation of sensory stimuli to create a meaningful and coherent understanding of the world. Perception is not simply the passive reception of sensory input but also includes the active process of selecting, organizing, and interpreting information based on previous experiences, expectations, and cognitive processes.

Perception involves various senses, including sight, hearing, touch, taste, and smell. It is a complex and dynamic process influenced by psychological, social, cultural, and individual factors. Our perception of the world is not always an accurate representation of objective reality; instead, it is often shaped by subjective factors and cognitive biases.

In summary, perception is the mental process of receiving, organizing, and interpreting sensory information to create a subjective understanding of the surrounding environment.

Impact of perception on our mindset

Perception plays a crucial role in shaping and influencing our mindset. The way we interpret and make sense of the world around us can significantly impact our thoughts, attitudes, and behaviors. Here are some key ways in which perception affects our mindset:

1. **Cognitive Framework:** Perception forms the foundation of our cognitive framework. The way we perceive information shapes the mental structures we use to understand and categorize the world. This framework influences how we process new information and make decisions.

2. **Belief Systems:** Our perceptions contribute to the formation of belief systems. What we see, hear, and experience can shape our beliefs about ourselves, others, and the world. These beliefs, in turn, influence our attitudes, values, and expectations.

3. **Cognitive Biases:** Perception is susceptible to various cognitive biases, which are systematic patterns of deviation from norm or rationality in judgment. Biases such as confirmation

bias, where we tend to favor information that confirms our preexisting beliefs, can significantly impact our mindset by reinforcing certain perspectives and limiting openness to alternative viewpoints.

4. **Emotional Responses:** Perception is closely linked to emotions. How we perceive situations and events can evoke emotional responses, affecting our overall emotional well-being. For example, a positive perception of challenges as opportunities for growth can lead to a more optimistic mindset.

5. **Social Interactions:** Perceptions of others and how we believe others perceive us can shape our social interactions. Positive perceptions can enhance social connections, while negative perceptions may lead to social withdrawal or conflict.

6. **Problem-Solving and Decision-Making:** Our perception influences how we approach problem-solving and decision-making. Different perceptions of the same situation can lead to different decisions and actions. A positive mindset, for instance, may encourage proactive problem-solving and resilience in the face of challenges.

7. **Self-Concept:** How we perceive ourselves, our abilities, and our worth contributes to our self-concept. Positive self-perception can foster confidence and motivation, while negative self-perception may lead to self-doubt and a more pessimistic mindset.

8. **Adaptability:** Perception is linked to our ability to adapt to new situations and challenges. A flexible and open-minded perception allows for greater adaptability, while rigid or negative perceptions can hinder the ability to adjust to changing circumstances.

In summary, perception is a fundamental aspect of our mental processes, influencing the way we think, feel, and interact with the world. Understanding and managing our perceptions can be essential for cultivating a positive and adaptive mindset.

Negative impact of perception on our mindset

Negative perceptions can have a significant impact on our mindset, influencing our thoughts, emotions, and behaviors in detrimental ways. Here are some common negative effects of perception on mindset:

1. **Cognitive Biases:** Cognitive biases, such as confirmation bias, where individuals tend to favor information that confirms their existing beliefs, can lead to closed-mindedness and a

resistance to considering alternative perspectives. This can hinder intellectual growth and the development of a more nuanced mindset.

2. **Distorted Self-Image:** Negative perceptions of oneself, often influenced by factors such as low self-esteem or unrealistic societal standards, can contribute to a distorted self-image. This may result in feelings of inadequacy, self-doubt, and a pessimistic outlook on one's abilities and potential.

3. **Stress and Anxiety:** Perceiving situations as more threatening or challenging than they objectively are can contribute to stress and anxiety. Negative perceptions of events, especially if exaggerated or catastrophic, can lead to heightened emotional responses and a heightened sense of vulnerability.

4. **Social Isolation:** Negative perceptions of others or a fear of negative judgment can contribute to social anxiety and withdrawal. This may result in reduced social interactions, limiting opportunities for positive relationships and support networks.

5. **Limited Problem-Solving Abilities:** Negative perceptions can narrow one's focus and limit creative problem-solving. Pessimistic outlooks may lead to a belief that challenges are insurmountable, hindering the development of effective solutions.

6. **Reduced Resilience:** A negative perception of setbacks or failures can erode resilience. Individuals with a consistently negative mindset may be less likely to bounce back from challenges, viewing obstacles as permanent and pervasive.

7. **Impact on Physical Health:** Prolonged negative perceptions and stress can have physical health implications, contributing to issues such as increased cortisol levels, elevated blood pressure, and a weakened immune system.

8. **Impaired Decision-Making:** Negative perceptions can cloud judgment and lead to suboptimal decision-making. When influenced by fear, anxiety, or a generally pessimistic outlook, individuals may make decisions based on avoidance rather than thoughtful consideration of options.

9. **Impaired Interpersonal Relationships:** Negative perceptions of others can lead to misunderstandings, conflicts, and strained relationships. Prejudices, stereotypes, and unfounded

judgments can hinder the development of positive and meaningful connections with others.

10. **Self-Fulfilling Prophecy:** Negative perceptions can become self-fulfilling prophecies. If someone consistently believes they will fail or that others will reject them, this belief can influence their actions and behaviors in ways that contribute to the predicted outcomes.

Recognizing and challenging negative perceptions is essential for promoting a healthier mindset. Strategies such as cognitive restructuring, mindfulness, and seeking alternative perspectives can help mitigate the negative impact of perception on mindset.

How to remove negative perception effects from our mindset

Removing or mitigating the negative effects of perception from our mindset involves intentional and proactive efforts to shift thought patterns, beliefs, and behaviors. Here are some strategies to help foster a more positive and balanced mindset:

1. **Awareness and Mindfulness:**
   - Pay attention to your thoughts and recognize negative patterns.
   - Practice mindfulness to stay present and observe thoughts without judgment.

2. **Challenge Negative Thoughts:**
   - Actively question and challenge negative thoughts. Are they based on facts or assumptions?
   - Consider alternative, more positive interpretations of situations.

3. **Cognitive Restructuring:**
   - Identify and reframe negative thought patterns. Replace irrational or harmful thoughts with more rational and constructive ones.
   - Use positive affirmations to counteract negative self-talk.

4. **Seek Different Perspectives:**
   - Encourage yourself to consider alternative viewpoints and interpretations of situations.
   - Talk to others and gain insight into their perspectives to broaden your understanding.

5. **Focus on Solutions:**
   - Instead of dwelling on problems, shift your focus to finding solutions.
   - Break down challenges into manageable steps and set realistic goals.

6. **Build a Support System:**
   - Surround yourself with positive and supportive individuals.
   - Share your concerns with trusted friends, family, or a mental health professional.

7. **Practice Gratitude:**
   - Regularly acknowledge and express gratitude for positive aspects of your life.
   - Keep a gratitude journal to cultivate a more optimistic outlook.

8. **Set Realistic Expectations:**
   - Adjust your expectations to be more realistic and achievable.
   - Celebrate small victories and progress, even if it's incremental.

9. **Develop a Growth Mindset:**
   - Embrace challenges as opportunities for growth and learning.
   - View setbacks as temporary and see them as a chance to improve.

10. **Engage in Positive Activities:**
    - Participate in activities that bring you joy and satisfaction.
    - Cultivate hobbies and interests that contribute to a positive mindset.

11. **Limit Negative Influences:**
    - Reduce exposure to negative media or social media content.
    - Be mindful of the impact of negative influences on your mindset.

12. **Self-Compassion:**
    - Treat yourself with kindness and understanding, especially in times of difficulty.
    - Recognize that everyone makes mistakes, and self-compassion is key to personal growth.

13. **Professional Help:**
    - If negative perceptions significantly impact your well-being, consider seeking support from a mental health professional who can provide guidance and strategies.

Remember that changing mindset is a gradual process, and consistency in practicing these strategies is key. It's also important to be patient and compassionate with yourself during this journey toward a more positive and resilient mindset.

CHAPTER 13
IMPACT OF IMAGINATION ON OUR MINDSET

Imagination has a profound impact on our mindset, influencing the way we think, feel, and interact with the world. Here are several ways in which imagination can shape and contribute to our mindset:

Creativity and Innovation:

Imagination is the foundation of creativity. It allows us to generate new ideas, envision possibilities, and think outside the box.

A mindset fueled by imagination is more likely to embrace innovation and seek novel solutions to problems.

Problem-Solving Abilities:

Imagination enables us to visualize various scenarios and potential outcomes. This mental simulation aids in problem-solving by exploring different approaches and considering alternatives.

Individuals with a well-developed imagination may approach challenges with a more adaptive and flexible mindset.

Optimism and Positive Thinking:

Imagination can contribute to a positive mindset by allowing us to envision positive outcomes and possibilities.

Visualizing success or positive scenarios can foster optimism and resilience in the face of adversity.

Goal Setting and Planning:

Imagination plays a role in setting and envisioning future goals. It helps individuals create a mental roadmap for achieving their aspirations.

A mindset enriched with imagination is likely to be goal-oriented and forward-thinking.

Empathy and Understanding:

Imagination allows us to put ourselves in the shoes of others, fostering empathy and a deeper understanding of different perspectives.

A mindset that incorporates imaginative empathy is more open-minded and accepting of diversity.

Reducing Fear and Anxiety:

Imagination can be used to confront and overcome fears. Visualizing success or coping strategies can help reduce anxiety about future events.

Creative visualization and guided imagery are techniques that leverage imagination to manage stress and anxiety.

Enhanced Memory and Learning:

Imagination is closely linked to memory and learning. Creating mental images or associations helps in retaining and recalling information.

A mindset that actively engages the imagination may be more adept at learning and retaining knowledge.

Coping Mechanism:

Imagination can serve as a powerful coping mechanism in challenging situations. Creating mental images of a better future or alternative outcomes can provide comfort and motivation.

Imaginative thinking can help individuals reframe negative experiences and find meaning in adversity.

Personal Growth and Exploration:

Imagination encourages exploration and the pursuit of personal growth. It allows individuals to envision their ideal selves and aspire to continuous improvement.

A mindset that values imagination is more likely to embrace new experiences and opportunities for growth.

Enhanced Communication Skills:

Imagination contributes to effective communication by enabling individuals to convey ideas, stories, and concepts in engaging and vivid ways.

A mindset that values imaginative communication fosters better interpersonal connections.

Summary, imagination is a dynamic cognitive process that has far-reaching effects on mindset, influencing how we approach challenges, interact with others, and navigate our lives. Cultivating and harnessing the power of imagination can contribute positively to the development of a creative, resilient, and adaptive mindset.

NEGATIVE IMPACT OF IMAGINATION

While imagination generally has many positive impacts on our mindset, there are instances where it can have negative effects. Here are some potential negative impacts of imagination on mindset:

Excessive Worry and Anxiety:

An overactive imagination can lead to excessive worrying and anxiety. Imagining worst-case scenarios or catastrophizing about the future can contribute to heightened stress levels.

Rumination and Obsessive Thinking:

Imagination can sometimes lead to repetitive and obsessive thoughts, particularly if these thoughts are focused on negative experiences or outcomes. This rumination can contribute to a negative mindset.

Unrealistic Expectations:

Imagination may lead to the creation of idealized or unrealistic expectations. When reality doesn't align with these imagined scenarios, it can result in disappointment and a negative mindset.

Fear of the Unknown:

Imagining unknown or uncertain situations can lead to fear and apprehension. The mind may generate negative possibilities, even if they are unlikely, contributing to a mindset of fear or avoidance.

Self-Doubt and Negative Self-Talk:

Imagination can contribute to negative self-talk, creating scenarios in which one doubts their abilities or imagines failure. This can undermine self-confidence and contribute to a negative self-perception.

Escapism and Avoidance:

Excessive imagination may lead to a tendency to escape reality through daydreaming or fantasy. While some degree of escapism is normal, excessive avoidance of reality can hinder personal growth and problem-solving.

Stagnation and Resistance to Change:

Imagination that is fixated on the past or resistant to change can contribute to a mindset of stagnation. Resistance to adapting to new situations or considering alternative perspectives may impede personal and professional development.

Social Anxiety:

Imagining negative outcomes in social situations can contribute to social anxiety. Creating scenarios where one imagines judgment or rejection by others can impact confidence and hinder social interactions.

Perfectionism:

Imagination can contribute to the creation of idealized standards, leading to perfectionistic tendencies. Striving for perfection can result in constant dissatisfaction and a negative mindset when expectations are not met.

Emotional Distress:

Vivid imagination, particularly in response to emotionally charged events, can lead to emotional distress. Replaying negative scenarios in the mind can perpetuate feelings of sadness, anger, or resentment.

It's important to note that the impact of imagination on mindset can vary from person to person, and not everyone will experience these negative effects. Additionally, imagination itself is not inherently negative; it's the content and direction of our imaginative thoughts that can influence our mindset positively or negatively. Developing awareness of negative thought patterns and practicing strategies to redirect or manage these thoughts can be beneficial in mitigating the potential negative impact of imagination on mindset.

How to mitigate negative Impact of imagination

Mitigating the negative impacts of imagination from our mindset involves intentional strategies and practices aimed at redirecting or managing negative thought patterns. Here are some techniques that can help:

Mindfulness and Awareness:

Practice mindfulness to become more aware of your thoughts without judgment.

When negative thoughts arise, acknowledge them without getting caught up in them. This awareness is the first step to addressing and mitigating their impact.

Challenge Negative Thoughts:

Actively challenge and question negative thoughts. Ask yourself if they are based on facts or assumptions.

Consider alternative, more balanced perspectives and challenge the validity of overly negative or catastrophic thinking.

Cognitive Restructuring:

Identify negative thought patterns and replace them with more positive or realistic ones.

Use positive affirmations to counteract negative self-talk and reinforce healthier beliefs about yourself and your abilities.

Visualization for Positive Outcomes:

Use the power of imagination for positive visualization. Instead of dwelling on negative scenarios, vividly imagine successful outcomes and positive experiences.

Engage in creative visualization techniques to create mental images of desired future states.

Set Realistic Expectations:

Evaluate and adjust your expectations to be more realistic and achievable.

Recognize that perfection is rarely attainable, and allow yourself room for mistakes and growth.

Focus on the Present:

Practice staying present in the moment through mindfulness techniques.

Redirect your imagination away from future worries or past regrets and focus on the current task or situation.

Cultivate a Growth Mindset:

Embrace challenges as opportunities for growth and learning.

View setbacks as temporary and consider the lessons they may offer for personal development.

Positive Self-Talk:

Replace negative self-talk with positive and affirming statements.

Encourage yourself as you would a friend, and be mindful of the language you use when thinking about yourself.

Limit Exposure to Negative Influences:

Be mindful of the media, social media, or individuals that contribute to negative thought patterns.

Limit exposure to content that reinforces negative imaginings and seek out positive and uplifting influences.

Seek Support:

Talk to friends, family, or a mental health professional about your concerns.

Sharing your thoughts and feelings with others can provide support, perspective, and guidance.

Engage in Relaxation Techniques:

Practice relaxation techniques such as deep breathing, meditation, or progressive muscle relaxation to calm the mind and reduce stress.

These techniques can help break the cycle of negative imagination associated with anxiety.

Focus on Solutions:

Instead of dwelling on problems, shift your focus to finding solutions.

Break down challenges into manageable steps and take action toward positive change.

Remember that changing thought patterns and mitigating the negative impact of imagination is a gradual process. Consistent practice of these techniques, along with patience and self-compassion, can contribute to a healthier and more positive mindset over time. If negative thoughts persist and significantly impact your well-being, seeking professional help may be beneficial.

CHAPTER 14
FIGURING OUT OURSELVES

"Figuring out ourselves" refers to the process of self-discovery and self-awareness. It involves gaining a deeper understanding of various aspects of our identity, including our thoughts, feelings, values, strengths, weaknesses, preferences, and overall personality. The process of figuring out ourselves often includes introspection, reflection, and exploration of our own experiences and behaviors.

This ongoing process allows individuals to become more conscious of who they are, what they want, and why they think or act in certain ways. It can involve questioning assumptions, examining personal beliefs, and identifying patterns in behavior. Figuring out ourselves is a dynamic and lifelong journey, as our understanding of ourselves evolves with new experiences, insights, and personal growth. This self-awareness can contribute to better decision-making, improved relationships, and a more authentic and fulfilling life.

IMPACT OF FIGURING OUT OURSELVES

The process of figuring out ourselves, or engaging in self-discovery and self-awareness, can have a profound impact on our mindset. Here are several ways in which this exploration influences our mindset:

Self-Acceptance:

Understanding our strengths, weaknesses, and unique qualities can lead to greater self-acceptance. Embracing who we are, without judgment, contributes to a more positive and compassionate mindset.

Clarity of Values:

Figuring out ourselves often involves identifying our core values and beliefs. When our actions align with these values, it can lead to a sense of purpose and contribute to a more focused and intentional mindset.

Increased Self-Efficacy:

Recognizing our capabilities and achievements builds self-efficacy, the belief in our ability to accomplish tasks. This positive mindset can lead to greater confidence and motivation to tackle challenges.

Emotional Regulation:

Understanding our emotional triggers and patterns allows us to regulate our emotions more effectively. This emotional intelligence contributes to a more balanced and resilient mindset.

Improved Decision-Making:

Self-discovery helps us understand our priorities and preferences, facilitating better decision-making. A clearer sense of self allows us to make choices that align with our values and long-term goals.

Adaptability:

A mindset shaped by self-discovery is often more adaptable. Awareness of our strengths and weaknesses allows us to navigate change more effectively and respond to challenges with resilience.

Authenticity in Relationships:

Knowing ourselves allows for more authentic and meaningful connections with others. Authenticity in relationships contributes to a positive and supportive social environment, impacting our mindset positively.

Reduced Self-Doubt:

Understanding our capabilities and limitations can reduce self-doubt. A mindset informed by self-discovery is more likely to approach challenges with confidence and a belief in one's ability to overcome obstacles.

Increased Motivation:

Identifying personal goals and aspirations provides motivation. A mindset shaped by self-discovery is often driven by a sense of purpose and the pursuit of personal growth and fulfillment.

Resilience in the Face of Setbacks:

Knowing ourselves enables us to develop resilience. When setbacks occur, a mindset grounded in self-awareness is better equipped to bounce back, learn from experiences, and maintain a positive outlook.

Enhanced Problem-Solving:

Understanding our thought processes and decision-making tendencies can lead to more effective problem-solving. A mindset informed by self-discovery is often open to innovative and creative solutions.

Mindfulness and Present Moment Awareness:

Figuring out ourselves often involves cultivating mindfulness and present moment awareness. This mindset encourages living in the present, reducing anxiety about the future or dwelling on the past.

Summary: The impact of figuring out ourselves on our mindset is significant and multifaceted. It contributes to self-acceptance, emotional well-being, improved relationships, and a more intentional and resilient approach to life's challenges. Engaging in ongoing self-discovery is a valuable investment in personal growth and the development of a positive mindset.

NEGATIVE IMPACT OF FIGURING OUT OURSELVES

While the process of figuring out ourselves generally has positive effects on our mindset, there can be certain challenges or negative impacts associated with this self-discovery journey. It's important to recognize these potential drawbacks to navigate the process more effectively:

Self-Criticism and Perfectionism:

Introspection can sometimes lead to heightened self-awareness, which may trigger self-criticism or perfectionistic tendencies. Becoming overly focused on perceived flaws can negatively impact self-esteem.

Overanalysis and Rumination:

Continuous self-analysis may lead to overthinking and rumination. Excessive dwelling on past actions or worrying about future decisions can contribute to stress and anxiety.

Identity Crisis:

Intensive self-reflection may raise questions about identity, purpose, and values. This can lead to a temporary sense of confusion or identity crisis as individuals reevaluate their beliefs and priorities.

Decision Paralysis:

Intense self-exploration can sometimes lead to indecision, especially if individuals become overly preoccupied with making the "perfect" choice. This can hinder progress and personal growth.

Comparison with Others:

Discovering aspects of ourselves might lead to comparisons with others. Unfavorable comparisons can contribute to feelings of inadequacy and negatively impact self-worth.

Overemphasis on Weaknesses:

Focusing excessively on weaknesses during self-discovery may overshadow strengths. This imbalance can contribute to a negative mindset and hinder the development of a more holistic self-view.

Resistance to Change:

Deep self-reflection might bring to light certain aspects of ourselves that we find uncomfortable. This can lead to resistance to change, as individuals may be reluctant to confront and address these aspects.

Strain on Relationships:

Intense self-exploration can influence relationships. For example, a partner or friend may find it challenging to understand or relate to shifts in behavior or values during the self-discovery process.

Loss of Naivety or Innocence:

Discovering certain truths about ourselves may result in the loss of naivety or innocence. While this can contribute to personal growth, it may also lead to a more cynical or jaded mindset.

Increased Sensitivity to Criticism:

Heightened self-awareness may make individuals more sensitive to criticism. Constructive feedback, which is essential for growth, may be perceived more negatively, impacting the mindset.

Feeling Overwhelmed:

The sheer depth and complexity of self-discovery can be overwhelming for some individuals. This overwhelm may lead to stress, anxiety, or a sense of being lost.

It's important to approach the process of figuring out ourselves with balance and self-compassion. Recognizing potential challenges and seeking support, whether from friends, family, or mental health professionals, can help navigate the negative impacts and foster a healthier self-discovery journey.

HOW TO REMOVE NEGATIVE IMPACT
OF FIGURING OUT OURSELVES

If you find that the process of figuring out yourself is having a negative impact on your mindset and well-being, there are steps you can take to navigate this journey more positively. Here are some strategies to help mitigate the potential negative effects:

Practice Self-Compassion:

Be kind and understanding toward yourself. Acknowledge that the process of self-discovery is complex and that it's okay to have imperfections or uncertainties.

Set Realistic Expectations:

Understand that self-discovery is an ongoing process, and it's natural for your understanding of yourself to evolve over time. Avoid placing unrealistic expectations on yourself.

Focus on Strengths:

Balance your self-reflection by acknowledging and focusing on your strengths. Celebrate your achievements and positive qualities rather than dwelling solely on perceived weaknesses.

Limit Overthinking:

If you find yourself overanalyzing or ruminating, practice mindfulness techniques to bring your attention back to the present moment. Engage in activities that help redirect your focus.

Seek Professional Support:

If the process becomes overwhelming, consider seeking guidance from a mental health professional. A therapist can provide support, offer perspective, and help you navigate challenges more effectively.

Embrace Change Gradually:

If you're uncovering aspects of yourself that you want to change, do so gradually. Small, manageable steps toward personal growth are more sustainable and less likely to cause stress.

Cultivate Gratitude:

Foster a positive mindset by practicing gratitude. Focus on aspects of your life that you appreciate, and regularly reflect on the positive experiences you've had.

Build a Support System:

Share your thoughts and feelings with trusted friends or family members. A supportive network can provide encouragement, feedback, and a sense of connection during times of self-discovery.

Reframe Negative Thoughts:

Challenge and reframe negative thoughts that arise during the self-discovery process. Replace overly critical or pessimistic thoughts with more balanced and positive perspectives.

Engage in Self-Care:

Prioritize self-care activities that bring you joy and relaxation. Taking care of your physical and emotional well-being can contribute to a more positive mindset.

Accept Uncertainty:

Recognize that it's normal to experience uncertainty and ambiguity during the self-discovery process. Embrace the journey as an opportunity for growth rather than viewing uncertainties as failures.

Focus on the Present:

Instead of getting lost in future worries or past regrets, practice mindfulness to stay present. Cultivating an awareness of the present moment can alleviate anxiety associated with self-discovery.

Remember that the journey of figuring out yourself is unique to each individual, and it's normal to encounter challenges along the way. By approaching this process with patience, self-compassion, and a balanced perspective, you can help mitigate negative impacts and foster a more positive and constructive mindset.

CHAPTER 15
IDENTITY

Identity refers to the distinguishing characteristics or qualities that make an individual or entity recognizable and unique. It encompasses the totality of who or what someone or something is, including their personal attributes, traits, beliefs, values, and experiences. Identity can be multifaceted, encompassing aspects such as cultural, social, gender, ethnic, religious, and personal identity.

In the context of individuals, identity is often shaped by a combination of inherent factors, such as genetics and biology, as well as external influences, such as culture, society, and personal experiences. It is dynamic and can evolve over time as a person goes through different life stages and encounters various influences.

In a broader sense, identity can also refer to the characteristics and attributes that define a group, community, or organization, contributing to a sense of shared purpose or belonging. The concept of identity is complex and can be explored from various perspectives, including psychological, sociological, cultural, and philosophical viewpoints.

IMPACT OF IDENTITY

Identity has a significant impact on our mindset, shaping how we perceive ourselves and others, influencing our thoughts, beliefs, and behaviors. Here are several ways in which identity can affect our mindset:

Self-Perception: Our identity plays a crucial role in shaping how we see ourselves. It encompasses aspects such as personal achievements, values, and beliefs. A positive identity can contribute to high self-esteem and a sense of purpose, while a negative identity or internal conflicts may lead to self-doubt and lower self-esteem.

Social Identity: Our sense of identity is often tied to social groups we belong to, such as family, friends, ethnic or cultural groups, and communities. These social identities can influence our mindset by shaping our attitudes, values, and behaviors, as we often seek validation and acceptance from these groups.

Cognitive Filters: Our identity can act as a set of cognitive filters through which we interpret the world. This is often referred to as confirmation bias, where we tend to give more weight to information that aligns with our existing beliefs and identities. It can influence the way we perceive and process information.

Motivation and Goals: Identity can influence our motivation and the goals we set for ourselves. For example, someone who strongly identifies as an athlete may be motivated to excel in sports, while someone identifying as an artist may be driven to pursue creative endeavors. Our identity can shape our aspirations and guide our life choices.

Interactions with Others: Identity affects how we interact with others. Our perceived identity and the stereotypes associated with it can impact our relationships. Additionally, our understanding of our own identity can influence our communication style, empathy, and ability to relate to individuals from diverse backgrounds.

Resilience and Coping: During challenging times, a strong and positive identity can contribute to resilience. Individuals who have a strong sense of identity may be better equipped to cope with setbacks, as their self-concept provides a foundation for overcoming obstacles and adapting to change.

Cultural and Global Perspective: Cultural identity shapes our worldview and influences how we perceive and interact with people from different cultures. It can impact our openness to diversity, tolerance, and understanding of global issues.

Decision-Making: Our identity can play a role in decision-making, influencing choices related to career, relationships, and lifestyle. For instance, an individual strongly identifying with environmentalism may make decisions that align with eco-friendly values.

Understanding the impact of identity on our mindset is crucial for personal development, fostering empathy, and promoting positive interactions within diverse societies. Embracing a nuanced and inclusive view of identity can contribute to a more open-minded and accepting mindset.

NEGATIVE IMPACT OF IDENTITY

While identity can have positive effects on our mindset, it can also contribute to negative impacts, especially when certain aspects of identity lead to harmful thoughts, attitudes, or behaviors.

Here are some ways in which the negative aspects of identity can influence our mindset:

Stereotyping and Prejudice: Identifying strongly with a particular group can lead to stereotyping and prejudice. Prejudice involves preconceived negative attitudes toward individuals based on their perceived group identity. This can result in biased thinking and discriminatory behavior.

Identity Conflicts: If an individual holds conflicting identities or experiences tension between different aspects of their identity, it can lead to internal struggles, cognitive dissonance, and emotional distress. For example, conflicting cultural, religious, or social identities may create inner turmoil.

Social Comparison: Strong identification with a specific group can lead to social comparison, where individuals compare themselves to others within or outside their group. This can result in feelings of superiority or inferiority, fostering competition, jealousy, or low self-esteem.

Exclusion and Discrimination: A strong identification with a particular group may lead to the exclusion of individuals who do not share the same identity. This exclusionary mindset can contribute to discrimination, marginalization, and the reinforcement of social inequalities.

Identity-Based Stress: For individuals who belong to marginalized or stigmatized groups, their identity can be a source of stress. Experiencing discrimination, microaggressions, or societal biases based on aspects of their identity can negatively impact mental health and well-being.

Rigid Beliefs: Strong identification with a particular identity can sometimes lead to rigid beliefs and an unwillingness to consider alternative perspectives. This closed-mindedness can hinder personal growth, learning, and the ability to adapt to new information.

Identity Crisis: In some cases, individuals may experience an identity crisis, where they struggle to define or redefine their sense of self. This can lead to feelings of confusion, anxiety, and a lack of direction, affecting overall mental well-being.

In-group Favoritism: Strong identification with a specific group may lead to in-group favoritism, where individuals prioritize the interests and well-being of their own group over others. This can contribute to division, conflict, and hostility between different groups.

It's important to note that the negative impact of identity on mindset is not inherent to identity itself but often arises from how individuals perceive and navigate their identities in the context of social dynamics. Awareness, empathy, and an open-minded approach to understanding and appreciating diverse identities can help mitigate the negative effects and contribute to a more inclusive and positive mindset.

HOW TO MANAGE NEGATIVE IMPACT OF IDENTITY

Mitigating the impact of negative identity on your mindset involves a combination of self-reflection, cognitive restructuring, and fostering positive connections with others. Here are some strategies to help mitigate the negative impact of identity on your mindset:

Self-Reflection:

Awareness: Reflect on your own identity and be aware of any negative thoughts or beliefs associated with it. Recognize that identity is multifaceted, and there may be positive aspects that you can emphasize.

Question Assumptions: Challenge negative assumptions or stereotypes you may hold about yourself or others based on identity. Ask yourself where these beliefs come from and whether they are accurate and fair.

Cognitive Restructuring:

Challenge Negative Thoughts: Actively challenge and reframe negative thoughts related to your identity. Replace self-critical or prejudiced thoughts with more positive and constructive ones.

Emphasize Positive Aspects: Focus on the positive aspects of your identity and acknowledge your strengths, accomplishments, and values. Celebrate the diversity within your identity.

Seek Support:

Connect with Others: Share your experiences and thoughts with supportive friends, family members, or mentors. Sometimes, external perspectives can provide valuable insights and encouragement.

Professional Help: If negative thoughts about your identity are significantly impacting your well-being, consider seeking support from a mental health professional who can help you navigate these challenges.

Diversify Your Perspectives:

Expose Yourself to Diversity: Actively seek out diverse perspectives and experiences. Engage with people from different backgrounds, cultures, and identities to broaden your understanding and challenge stereotypes.

Educate Yourself: Learn more about the history, experiences, and contributions of different identity groups. Education can foster empathy and reduce negative stereotypes.

Cultivate a Positive Environment:

Positivity: Surround Yourself with Choose to spend time with people who uplift and support you. Create a positive environment that encourages self-acceptance and personal growth.

Limit Exposure to Negative Influences: Minimize exposure to environments or individuals that perpetuate negative stereotypes or contribute to a harmful mindset.

Develop Resilience:

Mindfulness and Meditation: Practices like mindfulness and meditation can help you build resilience and cope with negative thoughts. They promote self-awareness and a non-judgmental attitude toward your thoughts and feelings.

Set Realistic Goals: Establish realistic and achievable goals that align with your values and aspirations. Success in these areas can contribute to a more positive self-image.

Promote Inclusivity:

Advocate for Inclusion: Be an advocate for inclusivity and diversity within your community or workplace. Encourage open dialogue about identity and promote understanding.

Challenge Discrimination: If you witness discriminatory behavior or negative attitudes towards certain identities, consider addressing them respectfully and promoting a more inclusive environment.

Remember that personal growth is an ongoing process, and it's okay to seek support and guidance along the way. By actively working on changing negative thought patterns, fostering positive connections, and embracing diversity, you can mitigate the impact of negative identity on your mindset.

CHAPTER 16
STRESS

Stress is a physiological and psychological response to a perceived threat, challenge, or demand. It is the body's way of reacting to a situation and preparing to face a perceived danger or difficulty. Stress is a natural and adaptive response that can be triggered by various factors, including environmental pressures, life events, and internal thoughts or feelings.

When an individual encounters a stressor (a stress-inducing stimulus or situation), the body releases stress hormones such as cortisol and adrenaline. These hormones prepare the body for the "fight-or-flight" response, a survival mechanism that helps individuals cope with perceived threats. Physiological changes associated with stress include increased heart rate, heightened alertness, and the redirection of energy to essential functions.

While stress is a normal part of life and can be beneficial in certain situations, chronic or excessive stress can have negative effects on physical and mental health. Prolonged exposure to stressors without adequate coping mechanisms can contribute to conditions such as anxiety, depression, cardiovascular problems, and other health issues.

It's important to note that people can experience stress differently, and what is perceived as stressful varies from person to person. Additionally, stress can be influenced by a combination of external factors (e.g., work pressures, relationship challenges) and internal factors (e.g., individual perceptions, coping strategies). Strategies to manage stress often involve developing healthy coping mechanisms, practicing relaxation techniques, and addressing underlying sources of stress when possible.

IMPACT OF STRESS

Stress can have a profound impact on our mindset, influencing our thoughts, emotions, and behaviors. The effects of stress on the mind can vary from person to person and depend on factors such as the intensity and duration of the stressors, as well as individual coping mechanisms. Here are several ways in which stress can impact our mindset:

Cognitive Functioning:

Impaired Concentration and Memory: High levels of stress can interfere with concentration and short-term memory. Individuals may find it challenging to focus on tasks, make decisions, or remember information.

Negative Thought Patterns: Stress can contribute to negative thought patterns, including increased worry, self-doubt, and pessimism. It may also lead to a heightened perception of threats or difficulties.

Emotional Well-being:

Mood Changes: Stress often contributes to mood swings, irritability, and feelings of frustration or overwhelm. Individuals may experience heightened emotional reactivity and find it challenging to regulate their emotions.

Increased Anxiety and Tension: Chronic stress is associated with increased levels of anxiety. Persistent worries and feelings of tension can impact overall emotional well-being.

Physical Health:

Impact on Sleep: Stress can interfere with sleep patterns, leading to difficulties falling asleep or staying asleep. Poor sleep, in turn, can further exacerbate stress and negatively affect mood and cognitive function.

Physical Symptoms: Stress can manifest in physical symptoms such as headaches, muscle tension, gastrointestinal issues, and other stress-related ailments.

Behavioral Changes:

Changes in Coping Mechanisms: People under stress may resort to unhealthy coping mechanisms, such as overeating, substance abuse, or withdrawal from social activities. These behaviors can have further negative consequences on mental well-being.

Decreased Motivation: Chronic stress may contribute to a sense of fatigue and decreased motivation. Individuals may struggle to initiate or sustain activities they would normally enjoy.

Social and Interpersonal Impact:

Strained Relationships: Stress can contribute to interpersonal conflicts and strain relationships. Individuals under stress may have less patience, empathy, or emotional availability, affecting their interactions with others

Social Withdrawal: Some people may respond to stress by withdrawing from social activities, which can further contribute to feelings of isolation and loneliness.

Impact on Coping Strategies:

Coping Mechanism Effectiveness: Stress can influence the effectiveness of coping strategies. In some cases, individuals may engage in maladaptive coping mechanisms, which can perpetuate the cycle of stress and negatively impact mental health.

It's important to note that while stress can have negative effects, individuals also vary in their resilience and ability to cope with stress. Developing healthy coping mechanisms, practicing stress management techniques, and seeking support when needed are essential strategies for mitigating the impact of stress on the mindset. Additionally, addressing the underlying sources of stress can contribute to long-term mental well-being.

NEGATIVE IMPACT OF STRESS

Stress can have a profound impact on our mindset, influencing our thoughts, emotions, and behaviors. The effects of stress on the mind can vary from person to person and depend on factors such as the intensity and duration of the stressors, as well as individual coping mechanisms. Here are several ways in which stress can impact our mindset:

Cognitive Functioning:

Impaired Concentration and Memory: High levels of stress can interfere with concentration and short-term memory. Individuals may find it challenging to focus on tasks, make decisions, or remember information.

Negative Thought Patterns: Stress can contribute to negative thought patterns, including increased worry, self-doubt, and pessimism. It may also lead to a heightened perception of threats or difficulties.

Emotional Well-being:

Mood Changes: Stress often contributes to mood swings, irritability, and feelings of frustration or overwhelm. Individuals may experience heightened emotional reactivity and find it challenging to regulate their emotions.

Increased Anxiety and Tension: Chronic stress is associated with increased levels of anxiety. Persistent worries and feelings of tension can impact overall emotional well-being.

Physical Health:

Impact on Sleep: Stress can interfere with sleep patterns, leading to difficulties falling asleep or staying asleep. Poor sleep, in turn, can further exacerbate stress and negatively affect mood and cognitive function.

Physical Symptoms: Stress can manifest in physical symptoms such as headaches, muscle tension, gastrointestinal issues, and other stress-related ailments.

Behavioral Changes:

Changes in Coping Mechanisms: People under stress may resort to unhealthy coping mechanisms, such as overeating, substance abuse, or withdrawal from social activities. These behaviors can have further negative consequences on mental well-being.

Decreased Motivation: Chronic stress may contribute to a sense of fatigue and decreased motivation. Individuals may struggle to initiate or sustain activities they would normally enjoy.

Social and Interpersonal Impact:

Strained Relationships: Stress can contribute to interpersonal conflicts and strain relationships. Individuals under stress may have less patience, empathy, or emotional availability, affecting their interactions with others.

Social Withdrawal: Some people may respond to stress by withdrawing from social activities, which can further contribute to feelings of isolation and loneliness.

Impact on Coping Strategies:

Coping Mechanism Effectiveness: Stress can influence the effectiveness of coping strategies. In some cases, individuals may engage in maladaptive coping mechanisms, which can perpetuate the cycle of stress and negatively impact mental health.

It's important to note that while stress can have negative effects, individuals also vary in their resilience and ability to cope with stress. Developing healthy coping mechanisms, practicing stress management techniques, and seeking support when needed are essential strategies for mitigating the impact of stress on the mindset. Additionally, addressing the underlying sources of stress can contribute to long-term mental well-being.

HOW TO MITIGATE NEGATIVE IMPACT OF STRESS

Mitigating the negative impact of stress involves adopting effective coping strategies and making lifestyle changes to promote overall well-being. Here are some practical ways to mitigate the negative impact of stress:

Practice Stress Management Techniques:

Deep Breathing and Relaxation: Engage in deep breathing exercises or progressive muscle relaxation to calm the nervous system and reduce tension.

Mindfulness and Meditation: Incorporate mindfulness or meditation practices into your routine to promote present-moment awareness and relaxation.

Exercise Regularly:

Physical Activity: Regular exercise has been shown to reduce stress hormones and trigger the release of endorphins, which are natural mood lifters. Find activities you enjoy, whether it's walking, jogging, yoga, or other forms of exercise.

Prioritize Sleep:

Establish a Routine: Maintain a consistent sleep schedule by going to bed and waking up at the same time each day. Create a calming bedtime routine to signal to your body that it's time to wind down.

Create a Comfortable Environment: Ensure your sleep environment is conducive to rest—keep the room dark, quiet, and at a comfortable temperature.

Healthy Lifestyle Choices:

Balanced Nutrition: Eat a well-balanced diet with a focus on whole foods, fruits, vegetables, and lean proteins. Avoid excessive caffeine and sugar intake, as they can contribute to stress and anxiety.

Hydration: Stay hydrated by drinking enough water throughout the day. Dehydration can exacerbate feelings of fatigue and stress.

Time Management:

Prioritize Tasks: Break down tasks into smaller, more manageable steps, and prioritize them. Focus on completing one task at a time rather than feeling overwhelmed by a long to-do list.

Set Realistic Goals: Establish realistic goals and expectations for yourself. Avoid setting excessively high standards that may contribute to stress.

Social Support:

Connect with Others: Share your feelings with friends, family, or a trusted confidant. Social support can provide emotional comfort and perspective.

Build a Support System: Cultivate a network of supportive relationships. Knowing that you have people to turn to in times of stress can be comforting.

Mind-Body Techniques:

Yoga and Tai Chi: Practices like yoga and tai chi combine physical movement with mindfulness, promoting relaxation and stress reduction.

(Tai chi is an internal Chinese martial art practiced for self-defense and health. Known for its slow, intentional movements, tai chi has practitioners worldwide and is particularly popular as a form of gentle exercise and moving meditation, with benefits to mental and physical health)

Biofeedback: Explore biofeedback techniques that provide real-time information about physiological responses to stress, helping you learn to control them.

(Biofeedback is the technique of gaining greater awareness of many physiological functions of one's own body by using electronic or other instruments, and with a goal of being able to manipulate the body's systems at will.)

Limit Stimulants and Screen Time:

Reduce Stimulants: Limit the consumption of stimulants such as caffeine, especially in the hours leading up to bedtime.

Screen Time Management: Minimize screen time, especially before bedtime. The blue light emitted by screens can interfere with sleep.

Seek Professional Support:

Therapy: Consider seeking therapy or counseling to explore and address the underlying causes of stress. Cognitive-behavioral therapy (CBT) is a particularly effective approach for stress management.

Medical Consultation: If stress is significantly impacting your physical or mental health, consult with a healthcare professional to rule out any underlying medical conditions and explore appropriate interventions.

Create Healthy Boundaries:

Learn to Say No: Set boundaries and learn to say no to additional commitments when you feel overwhelmed.

Delegate Responsibilities: Delegate tasks when possible and share responsibilities with others to avoid taking on too much.

Remember that managing stress is an ongoing process, and it's essential to incorporate a combination of these strategies into your lifestyle. Experiment with different approaches to find what works best for you, and be proactive in addressing stressors before they become overwhelming. If stress persists or becomes unmanageable, seeking professional guidance is a wise step toward developing effective coping mechanisms.

CHAPTER 17
EVENTS OF PAST, PRESENT AND FUTURE

The impact of events from the past, present, and anticipated future can significantly influence our mindset. Our mindset encompasses the attitudes, beliefs, and perspectives that shape how we interpret and respond to the world. Here's a breakdown of how events in each time frame can affect our mindset:

Past Events:

Memory and Perception:

Past events contribute to our memory and shape our perception of the world. Positive experiences may foster an optimistic mindset, while negative or traumatic events can lead to negative thought patterns.

Resilience or Trauma:

Our response to past events, especially challenges and adversity, can contribute to the development of resilience or, in the case of severe trauma, may influence our mindset with lingering negative effects.

Learning and Growth:

Reflecting on past events provides opportunities for learning and personal growth. Positive outcomes can instill confidence, while mistakes or setbacks can offer valuable lessons.

Present Events:

Emotional State:

Current events can have an immediate impact on our emotional state. Positive experiences can elevate mood, while stressors or challenges may induce feelings of anxiety, frustration, or joy.

Mindfulness:

Being present in the moment allows for a more mindful mindset. Engaging fully in current experiences, whether positive or challenging, can influence our overall sense of well-being.

Coping Strategies:

The strategies we employ to navigate present events contribute to our mindset. Effective coping mechanisms enhance resilience, while maladaptive strategies may perpetuate stress or negative thought patterns.

Future Anticipation:

Goals and Aspirations:

Anticipating the future shapes our goals and aspirations. Positive expectations can foster a hopeful and motivated mindset, while uncertainty or fear of negative outcomes may lead to anxiety.

Planning and Preparedness:

Preparing for the future can influence our mindset. A sense of preparedness and proactive planning can instill confidence, while a lack of preparation may contribute to anxiety or uncertainty.

Optimism or Pessimism:

Anticipating positive outcomes contributes to an optimistic mindset, while anticipating negative outcomes may lead to pessimism. Our beliefs about the future can impact our current attitudes and behaviors.

Interconnectedness:

Feedback Loop:

Past events can influence present thoughts and behaviors, which, in turn, shape future experiences. This interconnectedness creates a feedback loop where each time frame interacts with and influences the others.

Adaptability:

The ability to adapt and reframe our mindset in response to changing circumstances is crucial. A growth mindset, characterized by adaptability and a willingness to learn, can positively influence how we approach past, present, and future events.

Understanding the interconnected impact of past, present, and future events on our mindset allows for greater self-awareness. Cultivating a balanced and adaptive mindset involves acknowledging the influence of each time frame and actively working towards positive perspectives and coping strategies.

NEGATIVE IMPACT OF EVENTS OF PAST, PRESENT AND FUTURE

The negative impact of events from the past, present, and anticipated future can significantly affect our mindset. Here's how each time frame can contribute to negative influences on our mindset:

Past Events:

Trauma and Residual Effects:

Past traumatic events can leave lasting emotional scars and contribute to negative thought patterns. The residual effects of trauma may include anxiety, depression, and difficulties in forming trusting relationships.

Regret and Guilt:

Events from the past that involve mistakes or regrettable actions can lead to feelings of guilt and shame. Dwelling on past errors can contribute to a negative self-image and impact current decision-making.

Rumination:

Constantly replaying negative events from the past in our minds, a process known as rumination, can lead to overthinking and an increased susceptibility to anxiety and depressive feelings.

Present Events:

Stress and Overwhelm:

Current stressors, whether related to work, relationships, or other life challenges, can contribute to feelings of overwhelm. Persistent stress can negatively impact mental health and lead to a pessimistic mindset.

Adversity and Coping Challenges:

Facing adversity in the present can pose significant challenges. Difficulty in coping with stressors may contribute to a negative mindset, affecting one's outlook on life and future possibilities.

Negative Influences:

Present influences, such as exposure to negative environments or relationships, can shape our mindset. Toxic relationships, for example, can contribute to feelings of inadequacy, self-doubt, and negativity.

Future Anticipation:

Anxiety and Fear of the Unknown:

Anticipating negative outcomes in the future can lead to anxiety and fear. Worrying about potential challenges or catastrophizing possible scenarios can contribute to a pessimistic mindset.

Uncertainty and Lack of Control:

A sense of uncertainty about the future, especially when accompanied by a perceived lack of control, can contribute to feelings of powerlessness and anxiety, impacting one's mindset.

Catastrophic Thinking:

Catastrophic thinking involves imagining the worst-case scenarios for the future. This type of thinking can contribute to heightened stress levels and a negative outlook on what lies ahead.

Interconnectedness:

Negative Feedback Loop:

Negative events from the past, present challenges, and anticipated future difficulties can create a negative feedback loop. Each time frame can reinforce negative thoughts, emotions, and behaviors, leading to a self-perpetuating cycle.

Rigid Mindset:

Experiencing negative events in the past and present can contribute to the development of a rigid mindset. This rigidity may make it challenging to adapt to new circumstances and opportunities.

Addressing the negative impact of past, present, and future events on mindset involves adopting strategies for resilience, self-reflection, and coping. Seeking support from mental health professionals, developing healthy coping mechanisms, and practicing mindfulness can be essential in mitigating the negative influences and promoting a more positive and adaptive mindset.

HOW TO MITIGATE IMPACT OF EVENTS OF PAST, PRESENT AND FUTURE

Mitigating the impact of events from the past, present, and future on your mindset involves adopting a proactive and positive approach to managing challenges and fostering resilience. Here are some strategies you can consider:

Mindfulness and Present Moment Awareness:

Practice mindfulness to stay grounded in the present moment.

Focus on what you can control right now, rather than dwelling on the past or worrying about the future.

Acceptance:

Acknowledge and accept events from the past that you cannot change.

Recognize that some things are beyond your control, and it's okay not to have all the answers.

Learn from the Past:

Extract lessons from past experiences to facilitate personal growth.

Use mistakes as opportunities for learning and improvement.

Positive Reframing:

Reframe negative thoughts into positive ones.

Instead of dwelling on challenges, focus on potential solutions and opportunities for growth.

Set Realistic Goals:

Establish achievable goals based on your present circumstances.

Break larger goals into smaller, manageable steps to make progress more feasible.

Cultivate Resilience:

Develop resilience by building a strong support system.

Foster adaptability and the ability to bounce back from setbacks.

Self-Compassion:

Be kind to yourself during difficult times.

Avoid self-blame and recognize that everyone faces challenges.

Limit Future Worry:

Plan for the future, but avoid excessive worry.

Focus on preparing for future events within your control, and let go of unnecessary anxiety.

Seek Professional Support:

If past events continue to significantly impact your mental well-being, consider seeking support from a therapist or counselor.

Build a Positive Environment:

Surround yourself with positive influences.

Engage in activities and relationships that contribute to a positive mindset.

Gratitude Practice:

Cultivate gratitude by reflecting on positive aspects of your life.

Keep a gratitude journal to focus on the good things, even in challenging times.

Stay Flexible:

Be adaptable and open to change.

Understand that life is dynamic, and being flexible can help you navigate uncertainties more effectively.

Healthy Lifestyle:

Maintain a healthy lifestyle with regular exercise, balanced nutrition, and sufficient sleep.

Physical well-being can positively impact mental resilience.

Remember that everyone's journey is unique, and it's okay to seek professional help if needed. Integrating these strategies into your daily life can contribute to a more positive and resilient mindset.

CHAPTER 18
HOW TO TACKLE MINDSET

Mastering the mindset is a profound journey, an exploration of the intricate terrain of our thoughts and beliefs. It begins with an embrace of the present moment, a practice of mindfulness that anchors us in the here and now. This mindfulness serves as a compass, guiding us away from the pull of past regrets and the anxious grip of an uncertain future.

Acceptance becomes our ally, as we confront the realities of our past, present, and future without judgment. It's not about resignation but a conscious choice to make peace with our circumstances. The past, a teacher rather than an anchor, holds lessons that shape our understanding and foster growth.

Running, much like the journey of the mind, is a rhythmic dance of endurance and resilience. As your feet pound against the earth, so do your thoughts echo in the corridors of your mind. Tackling the mind is not a sprint; it's a marathon that requires mindful strides and intentional pacing.

Just as a runner tunes into their body, a mindful individual tunes into their thoughts. It's about acknowledging the rhythm of your mental footsteps, understanding the terrain of your emotions, and navigating the winding trails of your well-being. In the same way, a runner must be attuned to their breath, a mindful individual must breathe through the highs and lows of their mental landscape.

Emotions are the hills and valleys of the mind's marathon. You can't avoid them, but you can learn to navigate their peaks and descents. Like adjusting your pace on an uphill climb, managing emotions involves finding the right balance – neither rushing nor resisting. It's about embracing the steady flow of emotions, acknowledging their presence, and allowing them to pass like the scenery unfolding along a running route.

The mind, much like a runner's body, requires regular care. Just as you stretch before a run, mental well-being demands moments of stillness and introspection. Running is not just about the physical act; it's a holistic experience that encompasses the mind, body, and soul. Similarly, nurturing mental well-being involves not just managing thoughts and emotions but creating a space for self-reflection and renewal.

As you clock in miles, you build physical strength; as you tend to your thoughts and emotions, you cultivate mental resilience. Running through the landscape of your mind is a journey of self-discovery, a marathon where every step is an opportunity to learn, grow, and evolve. So, lace up your mental running shoes, breathe in the present moment, and embark on the run that is the exploration of your own mind.

Our past experiences, both positive and negative, hold valuable lessons. Tackling the mindset involves viewing the past not as an anchor but as a teacher. Every mistake, failure, or success is an opportunity for learning and growth. By extracting wisdom from our history, we equip ourselves with the tools to navigate present challenges and shape a more empowered future.

The stories we tell ourselves have a profound impact on our mindset. Positive reframing is the art of shifting our perspective from a problem-centric view to a solution-oriented one. Instead of seeing obstacles as insurmountable, we learn to view them as stepping stones to personal development. By reframing our narrative, we cultivate resilience and optimism.

Tackling the mind involves taking care of your thoughts, emotions, and mental well-being.

Here's a simple way to approach this:

Understand Your Thoughts: Just like how you tidy up your room, try to organize your thoughts. Notice what you're thinking and why. Are your thoughts making you feel happy or worried? Sometimes, thoughts can be like a story in your head. Try to see if they're helping you or making you feel upset.

Take Breaks and Rest: Your mind is like a muscle; it needs breaks to work well. Resting is essential. Like when you play a game or do your homework, your mind needs breaks too. Take time to relax, play, or do something you enjoy.

Talk About Your Feelings: It's okay to talk about how you feel. Just like sharing a secret with a friend, sharing your feelings can help you feel better. Find someone you trust—a family member, friend, or a teacher—and share your feelings with them. It can make a big difference.

Do Things that Make You Happy: Similar to how you eat your favorite food or play your favorite game because it makes you happy, do things that bring you joy. It could be drawing, playing, reading, or spending time with loved ones. Doing things that make you happy helps your mind feel good.

Practice Relaxation: Sometimes, your mind can feel like a busy road. You can calm it down with relaxation. Take deep breaths, do some easy exercises, or simply sit quietly for a few minutes. This can help your mind feel peaceful and clear.

Learn and Explore: Like you learn new games or discover new places, you can also learn new things. Keep your mind active by exploring new hobbies, reading new books, or trying new activities. Learning keeps your mind curious and engaged.

Remember, taking care of your mind is like taking care of a garden. Just like you water plants and remove weeds to help them grow, taking care of your mind helps you grow and be your best self.

Let's dive into a little story to make these concepts more relatable:

Once there lived a wise elder named Grandpa Owen. He was known throughout the village for his storytelling prowess and the wisdom he had gained through the ebb and flow of his own life.

One day, curious young Mia approached Grandpa Owen and asked, "Grandpa, is life more about joys or sorrows?"

Grandpa Owen, with a twinkle in his eye, beckoned Mia to sit beside him on the weathered bench outside his cozy cottage. "Life, my dear Mia, is like a bundle of twine," he began, holding up a spool of twine for emphasis.

"Now, imagine each twist of this twine as a moment in your life. Some twists are bright and colorful, like the joys that make your heart dance. Perhaps it's the laughter of friends, the warmth of the sun on your face, or the thrill of discovering something new."

Mia nodded, captivated by the imagery. "But, Grandpa, what about the dark twists, the sorrows?"

Grandpa Owen nodded knowingly. "Ah, yes, the sorrows. They are the shadows that dance with the light. Picture the twine continuing to unwind. There are knots, tangles, and moments that bring tears. It might be a farewell, a dream that slips away, or a heart that feels heavy with loss."

As Grandpa Owen spoke, Mia's gaze shifted between the spool of twine and the wrinkles etched on his kind face.

"But, my dear," Grandpa continued, "here's the magic of life. The joys and sorrows aren't separate; they're intertwined. See, when the twine takes a darker turn, it makes the bright moments stand out even more. The contrast is what makes the tapestry of life beautiful and rich."

With a gentle smile, he handed Mia the spool of twine. "Hold onto it, my dear. Embrace each twist, whether it brings laughter or tears. For it's in the dance of joy and sorrow that you truly experience the fullness of life."

As Mia left Grandpa Owen's cottage, twine in hand, she carried with her a newfound understanding. Life, she realized, wasn't about avoiding the sorrows or seeking only the joys. It was about embracing the entire bundle, appreciating the intricate weave of moments that created the unique and beautiful tapestry of her life. And so, with each twist and turn, Mia walked forward, ready to unravel the bundle of sorrows and joys that lay ahead.

In conclusion, mastering the mindset is a continuous and dynamic journey. It is not a destination but a process of self-discovery, growth, and resilience. By embracing the present, learning from the past, and planning for the future with intention and mindfulness, we can navigate the maze of the mindset with purpose and grace. The transformation is not a one-time event but a lifelong commitment to cultivating a mindset that empowers, uplifts, and fosters a deep sense of well-being. As we embark on this transformative journey, we realize that the power to shape our mindset lies within, waiting to be uncovered and harnessed for a life of fulfillment and purpose.

In the realm of the human mindset, twining, interlacing, and embracing can be understood as symbolic gestures reflecting the intricate dynamics of thoughts, emotions, and relationships:

Twining of Thoughts:

The twining of thoughts represents the way ideas and mental processes can intertwine and collaborate. It's the weaving together of different strands of thought to form a cohesive understanding or perspective. Just as climbing plants seek support and stability by twining around structures, our thoughts can find strength and clarity through interconnectedness.

Interlacing of Emotions:

Interlacing emotions involves the intricate weaving of different feelings and sentiments. Human emotions are complex and multifaceted, often interwoven in a way that creates a rich tapestry of experience. Like the threads of a fabric coming together to form a pattern, our emotions blend and interact, shaping our overall emotional landscape.

Embracing Relationships:

Embracing in a human context goes beyond the physical act of hugging; it extends to the emotional and psychological connection with others. It symbolizes the mutual support, understanding, and acceptance within relationships. The intertwining of lives, experiences, and aspirations creates a bond that is resilient and nurturing.

Furthermore, embracing can also signify an open-minded approach to diverse perspectives and ideas. It involves a willingness to accept and integrate different viewpoints, fostering a sense of unity and collaboration in the broader human experience.

In the human mindset, these acts reflect the interconnected nature of our internal world and our relationships with others. The twining of thoughts and interlacing of emotions contribute to the complexity of our individual experiences, while the embracing of relationships and diverse perspectives adds depth and richness to the collective human tapestry. Just as in nature and crafts, these mental processes highlight the beauty and strength that emerge from the thoughtful intertwining of various elements in the human mind.

In conclusion, mastering the mindset is a continuous and dynamic journey. It is not a destination but a process of self-discovery, growth, and resilience. By embracing the present, learning from the past, and planning for the future with intention and mindfulness, we can navigate the maze of the mindset with purpose and grace. The transformation is not a one-time event but a lifelong commitment to cultivating a mindset that empowers, uplifts, and fosters a deep sense of well-being. As we embark on this transformative journey, we realize that the power to shape our mindset lies within, waiting to be uncovered and harnessed for a life of fulfillment and purpose.